The Effective Organization

The Effective Organization

The Nuts and Bolts of Business Value

Lee Schlenker
Alan Matcham

John Wiley & Sons, Ltd

Email (for orders and customer service enquiries): cs-books@wiley.co.uk
Visit our Home Page on www.wiley.com

Other Wiley Editorial Offices

John Wiley & Sons Inc., 111 River Street, Hoboken, NJ 07030, USA

Jossey-Bass, 989 Market Street, San Francisco, CA 94103-1741, USA

Wiley-VCH Verlag GmbH, Boschstr. 12, D-69469 Weinheim, Germany

John Wiley & Sons Australia Ltd, 33 Park Road, Milton, Queensland 4064, Australia

John Wiley & Sons (Asia) Pte Ltd, 2 Clementi Loop #02-01, Jin Xing Distripark, Singapore 129809

John Wiley & Sons Canada Ltd, 22 Worcester Road, Etobicoke, Ontario, Canada M9W 1L1

Wiley also publishes its books in a variety of electronic formats. Some content that appears
in print may not be available in electronic books.

Library of Congress Cataloging-in-Publication Data:

Schlenker, Lee.
   The effective organization : the nuts and bolts of business value / Lee
Schlenker, Alan Matcham.
      p. cm.
   Includes index.
   ISBN-13 978-470-02492-8
   ISBN-10 0-470-02492-5
1.   Organizational effectiveness.   2.   Value added.   3.   Information
technology – Economic aspects.   4.   Organizational change.   5.   Success in
business.   I. Title: Business value. II. Matcham, Alan. III. Title.
   HD58.9.S347 2005
   658.4'01 – dc22
                                                                    2004027308

British Library Cataloguing in Publication Data

A catalogue record for this book is available from the British Library

ISBN-13 978-470-02492-8 (HB)
ISBN-10 0-470-02492-5 (HB)

Typeset in 10/16pt Kuenstler by Laserwords Private Limited, Chennai, India
Printed and bound in Great Britain by TJ International, Padstow, Cornwall
This book is printed on acid-free paper responsibly manufactured from sustainable forestry
in which at least two trees are planted for each one used for paper production.

Contents

Foreword

Sergio Giacoletto – EVP Oracle EMEA

Most organizations today operate in a networked, highly connected environment where remaining competitive requires different strategies from those previously deployed. Information, knowledge, innovation and organizational flexibility are becoming the pillars of success as we enter an era where we move from the law of diminishing returns, based only on efficiency improvements, to the law of enriching returns, based on the information age and the knowledge economy.

We are witnessing a significant shift from delivering value through product functions and features to a service- and solution-based approach, a solution being defined here as a combination of products and services, together with the human touch that enables understanding, trust and relationships to develop. In this context responsibility for delivering real value today, particularly in the service industry, lies as much with people who manage relationships as it does with product experts.

I find it helpful to think of my own organization as a web of human interactions facilitated by a web of electronic connections. Value within the business is created from experience and passed from one person to another, one country to another and one industry to another.

In our search for greater flexibility we foster the development of social networks and less formal structures. Employees are encouraged to become members of several communities in order to stimulate the creation of innovative solutions to our clients' problems. However, there is always more one can do and that is why I welcome the contribution of this book.

Through this book, Lee Schlenker and Alan Matcham shed light on a number of critical points that enable the reader to reframe the way value can be created in today's business environment. Taking a range of examples, they begin by examining the inherent links between business value, business models and corporate strategy. They describe how the impact of ICT on management has influenced our perceptions of value and they propose the Business Value Matrix™ as a guide to determining how best to deploy talent, organization and technology to produce value.

I believe this book represents an important milestone in our understanding of how business value is evolving and addresses the challenge of business value whilst delivering tested strategies to build a more effective business organization.

Preface

*D*orothy,[1] *one of the guests on the 1950s television show, 'This is Your Life', explained that her 'job' over the preceding thirty years was attaching nuts to bolts. When the show's host, Groucho Marx, inquired what products her firm produced and the importance of her work, she readily admitted that she didn't know . . .*

Patrick, a sales development manager for a leading European hardware supplier, recently explained that his 'job' for the foreseeable future was producing 'euros and cents'. When we inquired as to how he planned on reaching this objective, he admitted that he really didn't know . . .

Over the last several decades customer demands for quality, for service and for value have changed significantly in both industry and commerce. During the same time span, management's formula for improving corporate productivity has remained 'quicker + cheaper = better'. Our firms today have never been so efficient, and yet our employees and managers complain of ever-increasing levels of apathy, stress and rigidity in our organizations. The following pages do not propose a quick fix for the 'efficiency' paradigm, but a fundamentally different vision of how we add value to our work and our organizations.

As a manager, your 'job' is adding value to your organization. Your competitive position in your company, in your profession and in your career is based on client perceptions of the value of the products and services you have to offer. Client perceptions of value have changed significantly over the years as the global economy has encouraged the progressive outsourcing of products, business processes and talent. Unfortunately, most of the management books you will read miss this point in just focusing on producing better products or more efficient organizations. In the pages that follow we will directly address the challenge of business value, and propose practical strategies to build an effective business organization.

This book is intended for all employees actively searching for the means to add measurable value to their careers and their organizations. Our objective is to explore with you the issues and challenges of leveraging information technology to respond more effectively to clients' needs and objectives both within your company and within your market. Based upon our own clients' successes and failures over the last decade, we hope that this contribution can provide a common forum for discussion within your organization and between your firm and its different business partners.

Exploring business value requires coming to grips with a number of issues. Let us begin by trying to ask the right questions:

- To what extent is business value the key indicator in determining success for both a manager and his or her organization?
- How has business value been influenced by the evolution of management wisdom over the last two decades?
- How has our perception of business value been formed and distorted by organizational and technological innovation?
- How can we broaden the focus of our employees, managers and business partners from efficiency gains to building more effective working relationships?

- What are the implications of the 'networked economy' on building business value today?
- What needs to be learned to put the ideas presented in this book into practice?

Several threads will be woven into the fabric of the chapters that follow. The first chapter will lay the foundations for our arguments in examining the inherent links between business value, business models and corporate strategy. We will contend that business value is fundamentally different from either performance or productivity. We demonstrate that the notion of business value has evolved significantly over the last 15 years. We argue that there is no 'one best way' for adding value to organizations; the search for business value is a perpetual quest that involves adapting physical and information resources to the evolving reality of distinct business communities. We conclude in proposing the Business Value Matrix™ as a guide to determining how we can best deploy talent, organization and technology to produce value in each organization and in each market.

The second chapter examines the complex relationship between recent innovations of information technology and the evolution of the practice of management. The impact of IT on management over the last two decades has been less a question of processing speed than how information technology has shaped, and been shaped by, new concepts of management, productivity and value. The last three decades have witnessed distinct revolutions in business information systems: the invention of the personal computer, the dissemination of relational databases, the development of client–server architectures and the introduction of the Internet have all tested deeply rooted beliefs on both how the firm should be structured and how value should be measured. The notion of 'personal' productivity, which directly threatened classical conceptions of industry and commerce in the late 1970s, has been contested in turn by new models of the value chain, of reengineering, of the extended enterprise and most recently by the networked economy. Since neither of these evolutions has replaced the others, all compete for management's attention in the corporate agenda.

If information technology helps us be 'quicker, cheaper and better', why are we not more productive? This productivity paradox is essentially due to the fact that we view information technology as both a measurement tool and a source of corporate performance. Business value is the result of a number of factors of production, as well as of the corporate vision of where the organization has been and where it would like to go. We will argue in the third chapter that 'productivity' depends not only on how we measure performance but on the information technology we use to do so. We will explore how good intentions concerning information technology often lead to poor business practice. We will conclude that the most significant contribution of information technology is not in its ability to precisely measure value, but in its capacity to push us to think differently about the relationship between what we measure and how we wish to improve our business practice.

The fourth chapter examines how the trend from producing products towards focusing on services and clients has impacted our perceptions of business value. We will begin this analysis with an overview of the evolution of 'process-centric' applications from enterprise resource planning to supply chain management to client relationship management. We will investigate how the client perceives value, and the extent to which clients contribute to value creation. We will examine how 'client-centric' approaches have challenged how we use IT to capture business value, where we attempt to improve processes, and what results we measure. We will conclude with a discussion of how these challenges can impact strategies for change management in your business.

The fifth chapter examines the role of IT in facilitating change in individuals, firms and markets. To what extent can technology-driven change be a catalyst for improving organizational performance? The dynamics of change have led in some cases to a virtuous circle reinforcing an organization's ability to respond to evolving market conditions, and in others to a vicious circle disrupting organizational focus, eroding competitive position and inevitably leading to problems with the bottom line. We will conclude this chapter with a discussion of why in certain cases IT appears to reinforce virtuous circles of creativity and passion, and in others leads to vicious circles of standardization, demotivation, and apathy towards work and the workplace.

In the sixth chapter of this work, we introduce the notion of the 'joined-up economy' as a vision for driving business value. In the last decade, innovative business executives have transformed their firms into networked businesses characterized by the 'digitalization' of key business processes, the integration of market norms for information exchange, the development of business communities around visions of shared benefits and the co-engineering of new market opportunities. In the next decade, business value in the joined-up economy will be tied to the ability to build bridges both between your organization and its market and between current practice and your vision of the future. How will information technology evolve to add value in this 'joined-up economy'?

The final chapter will explore what your managers and employees need to learn about using information technology to build business value, learning about business as a process integrated in your business community rather than in management theory of notions of best practice. The value of information technology is not in increasing the distance between employees, the organization and their customers, but in building bridges over culture, time and space to bring management and their clients together. Successful implementations use information technology to break down the physical and mental barriers between 'learning' and 'work' rather than pushing learning outside of the workplace or promoting quicker, cheaper, more efficient processes. Finally, successfully building a learning community depends upon designing information strategies that complement company culture and current technology investments.

In sum, we hope to share with you how our Business Value Matrix™ can help you breed business value into your projects, teams and organizations. The reality of the joined-up economy encourages us to focus on how we can work together with our clients and business partners to build business value. A new generation of information technology, based on collaborative strategies, can be used to capture, store and communicate new metrics on the effectiveness of our relationships with internal and external clients. Built upon the foundations of 'efficiency', a new mindset around effectiveness, talent and innovation can help provide the nuts and bolts of business value for your careers, professions and organizations.

Lee Schlenker   Ecole de Management de Lyon   lee@lhstech.com
Alan Matcham The Oracle Corporation alan.matcham@oracle.com
http://leeschlenker.typepad.com

Note

1. The stories that illustrate this work have been taken from real-life experience – certain names have been changed to help ensure anonymity.

Acknowledgements

O ne of the central ideas of this book is that business value is a product of human interaction. Nowhere has the reality of the 'joined-up economy' appeared clearer to us than in the support, advice and suggestions that we have received from our friends and colleagues in the preparation of this book.

There are many whose interviews and observations provided the backdrop for the work presented here. We would particularly like to thank Sergio Giacoletto and Juan Rada of the Oracle Corporation, David Burt of Deutsch Ltd, David Henshaw of Liverpool City Council, Dietmar Kirchner of Lufthansa, Kees Pronc of Microsoft, Rosemarie Dissler of Swiss Re and Philippe Vial of the Caisse d'Épargne.

As many readers will note, the ideas of John Seely Brown, Erik Brynjolfsson and Ralph Stacy have greatly influenced our thinking. David Mitchell and Toby Thompson have also made particularly important contributions. In acknowledging them specifically we do not ignore the help of many others who contributed in the development of our ideas. This said, we alone rest accountable for the pages to come.

We are also very grateful for the enthusiastic support of John Wiley & Sons Ltd. We thank in particular our energetic editor Sarah Booth, whose support and encouragement proved both efficient and effective, but also Rachel Goodyear, Lorna Skinner and Amelia Thompson whose logistical support was outstanding.

Last and certainly not least, we would like to underline the contributions, both directly and indirectly, of our wives and families. Their ideas, support and passion greatly surpasses anything we could put into words in this book, or any other.

Some of the work developed here has been presented elsewhere. In particular, Chapter 1 'In Search of Business Value' was initially prepared for the UKIAS 2004 conference, and the background material for Chapter 7 'Soldiers of the Shadows' was developed for various European Commission projects on the Information Society.

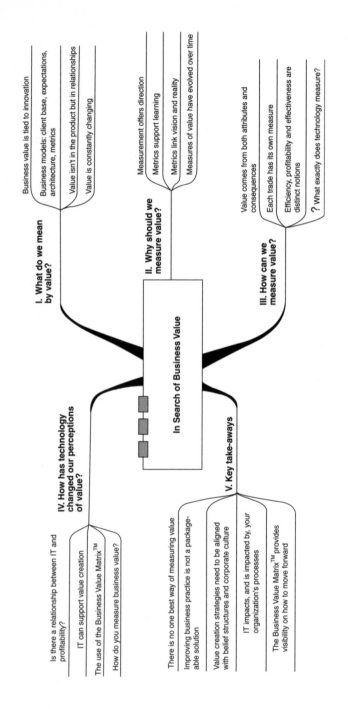

In Search of Business Value

I. What do we mean by value?
- Business value is tied to innovation
- Business models: client base, expectations, architecture, metrics
- Value isn't in the product but in relationships
- Value is constantly changing

II. Why should we measure value?
- Measurement offers direction
- Metrics support learning
- Metrics link vision and reality
- Measures of value have evolved over time

III. How can we measure value?
- Value comes from both attributes and consequences
- Each trade has its own measure
- Efficiency, profitability and effectiveness are distinct notions
- What exactly does technology measure?

IV. How has technology changed our perceptions of value?
- Is there a relationship between IT and profitability?
- IT can support value creation
- The use of the Business Value Matrix™
- How do you measure business value?

V. Key take-aways
- There is no one best way of measuring value
- Improving business practice is not a package-able solution
- Value creation strategies need to be aligned with belief structures and corporate culture
- IT impacts, and is impacted by, your organization's processes
- The Business Value Matrix™ provides visibility on how to move forward

1
In Search of Business Value

How Clear Is Your Picture of Business Value?

After a superb meal of local dishes at the Auberge de Talloires on the eastern bank of the lac d'Annecy, we retired to the drawing room for an after-dinner drink. The waiter suggested a 125-year-old bottle of Calvados as a perfect complement to the richly appointed atmosphere of this fourteenth-century abode. The eyes of our Scottish colleague, reflecting the intelligence, organization and mischief of thirty years of consulting for the IT industry, suddenly beamed in expectation of another treasured moment. He was not to be disappointed. He savoured the first taste, comparing this unique pleasure to previous experience. In his long career, he concluded, he had never experienced a clearer definition of value.

A manager's job is adding business value to his or her organization. In the preface to *The Value Enterprise* (Donovan *et al.*, 1998), the authors suggest that the most significant challenges facing management today are communicating clearly what they want their firms to become and how to get there. If we can come to grips with this apparent contradiction between management's quest for value and their apparent inability to share this vision with their employees, customers, business partners and shareholders, we will have taken a major step towards plotting a course for building business value in the future.

The following pages contest a number of commonly accepted management practices. We contend that business value is fundamentally different from either performance or productivity. We demonstrate that the notion of business value has evolved significantly over the last 15 years. We argue that there is no 'one best way' for adding value to organizations or to your careers. We conclude that the search for business value is a perpetual quest that involves applying talent, process and technology to the evolving reality of each business community.

To support our claims, let us explore a number of questions together:

- What do we mean by value, and what is the specificity of 'business value'?
- Why should we measure value, and why should we care about how we measure it?
- How can we measure value, and to what extent can technology facilitate this task?
- To what extent has the evolution of organization and technology changed the way we look at value?
- What are the paths of a roadmap to adding business value to our organizations?

What Do We Mean by Business Value?

Over the years economists have offered generally consistent views on 'value', 'profits' and 'business value'. *Value* is a product of labour and is captured in the price of goods and services that is itself set by the balance of supply and demand. Value may be defined as the essence of an organization's identity: why stakeholders (internal and external clients) choose to do business with that organization. *Profits* are surplus value derived from the proper allocation of capital and labour. *Business value* has been viewed as a characteristic of industrial innovation, while the function of management has been defined as maintaining competitive differentiation (Schumpeter, 1934). The advent of globalization of markets, technologies and organizations has increasingly provided managers with opportunities to become innovators in their own right, not in producing new products but in elaborating new strategies for value creation.

Simply put, companies invest in a product and/or service offer in the hope of receiving a proportionally greater return on their investment. If they succeed, they have created business value. Since most companies compete in markets with other firms offering similar products and services, creating sustainable business value is intimately linked to the coherence of the firm's business model over time. Business models, formulated either explicitly or implicitly, are built upon four cornerstones:

- *The client base*: How has the company targeted its client base and then segmented it by client needs and objectives?
- *Expected benefits*: What benefits are clients looking for in their relationship with the firm?
- *Process architecture*: How has the organization (human and technological resources) been designed to offer the products and services that meet clients' needs and objectives?
- *Metrics*: How is the organization measuring the revenues generated by these products and services in light of the market and the competition?

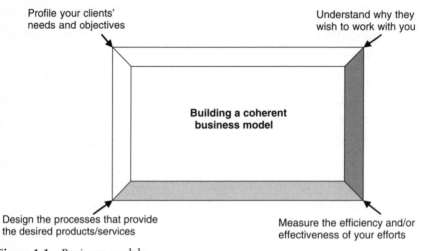

Figure 1.1 Business models

Several points can be underlined here. Business value does not come directly from either your products or your company; business value is determined by the relationship you nurture with your clients. Companies have internal (employees, managers and stockholders) and external (distributors, customers, regulatory agencies) clients, each with potentially differing needs and objectives. Clients' perceptions of value change over time, requiring companies to revise their business strategies to maintain their competitive advantage. Information technology plays several roles in shaping business value: it can help us understand this business challenge, enhance the advantages of our product/service offer, and measure and communicate the results of our efforts.

Why Measure Business Value?

Given the difficulty in understanding the roots of business value, it can be legitimately asked why we should go to the trouble of measuring it at all? As with the concepts of productivity, quality and learning, measurement systems reveal both what is actually produced within an organization and what can be done better.

In discussing productivity, Drucker underlined the importance of measurement: 'Without productivity objectives, a business does not have direction. Without productivity measurement, a business does not have control' (Drucker, 1974). In analysing quality, Deming argued that operational definitions give communicable meaning to concepts by specifying how the concept is measured and applied within a particular set of circumstances (Deming, 1982). Scott, Sink and Morris (1995) have in turn stressed the link between measurement and organizational learning in that 'measurement fosters organizational learning when management teams become skilled at converting data to information and information to knowledge'.

Management can provide a strong link between corporate vision and reality in developing operational measures of business value. Measures of business value are designed to promote three objectives: to raise awareness about what business value means to the organization, to establish guidelines to understand the relationships between business value, productivity and performance, and to identify a learning agenda to heighten the business value of future products and services.

How Have Measures of Business Value Evolved over Time?

Measures of business value have evolved over time with the evolution of markets and technologies. In the not-too-distant past, business value was directly associated with a firm's product offer. As a case in point, consider the invention of the Bic pen. In 1950, Marcel Bich created a revolutionary ball-point pen which he called Bic.[1] Ball-point, clear-barrelled, smooth-writing, non-leaky and inexpensive, the advantages of the 'Ball-point Bic' were clearly visible to consumers throughout the world. The product's characteristics were commonly perceived as 'better' value than anything else on the market. As a result, the future Baron Bich built his company in 1953 to 'develop the machines and the industrial processes needed to produce this innovative product and assure its high quality'.

Can the same be said of most products today? Is the value of Chanel No. 5 perfume, Michelin tyres, or the A380 jet in the products themselves or in the information and services that are packaged with the product? On what criteria do we purchase perfume, tyres or aeroplanes? Why do we choose one 'product' rather than another? Are the firms Chanel, Michelin and Airbus Industries structured to produce the machines and industrial processes needed to manufacture these products or organized to service the brand and its market? To what extent do these companies design, manufacture, distribute and service their own products? Is the business value of these companies in their products, in their organization, or in the relationships they maintain with their clients?

It can be argued convincingly that the nature of business value has evolved significantly over the last several decades. For products ranging from tennis shoes to higher education, the importance of criteria such as price, reliability, performance and technology have given way to privileging brand name, service, packaging and appearance. In an era of shopping centres and web stores, the importance of product knowledge, maintenance and proximity has given way to client perceptions of reputation, responsiveness and service.

	From the value of products . . .	. . . to business value
Intrinsic (Product)	Performance	Appearance
	Price	Brand name
	Reliability	Styling
	Technology	Packaging
Extrinsic (Vendor)	Operator training	Context
	Maintenance training	Reputation
	Parts	Reliability
	Post-purchase costs	Responsiveness
	Warranty	Service

Figure 1.2 Elements of business value

How Do We Add Value to a Company Today?

Empirically, the relationship between a firm's financial performance and its stock price is becoming increasingly difficult to demonstrate. A company's non-financial performance now plays a critical role in how the company is evaluated: strategy, execution, management experience and attractiveness are currently accepted measures of performance. As a result, investments in brand development, training and R&D now exceed total investments in tangible assets. The accounting firm Cap Gemini Ernst & Young concludes that at least a third of a mature company's value is attributable to non-financial information. For small and medium-sized companies, the proportion is even larger (Low and Cohen Kalafut, 2002).

In a similar vein, the relationship between a product's cost and the customer's perception of the value of a vendor relationship has steadily diminished. Loyalty to a brand or a vendor is increasingly dependent on a number of cost factors not directly associated with either specific products or services. These include:

- the nature of the relationship/business model with the supplier or vendor;
- acquisition/purchasing and decision-making processes;
- supplier capability, consistency and dependability;
- learning, knowledge and information transfer and solution development.

In this light, to what extent does business value depend on a firm's ability to manufacture, sell and service its own products? From a customer's perspective, product or service differentiation becomes increasingly more difficult, not only because of diminishing differences in technology and performance, but because productivity gains from one vendor to another have become increasingly marginal over time. In sharp contrast to the formulas for success fifty years ago, improving the machines and processes needed to manufacture the firm's products may be less a guarantee of adding business value than efforts devoted to improving the quality of client relationships.

How Do We Measure Value?

Is what you measure what you get? From a customer's point of view, value is measured in a number of ways. We refer to *attribute-based* value when a customer privileges a product's characteristics or functions. Marketing specialists have also referred to *consequence-based* value when customers identify value with their perceptions of the impact of their use of a product on their own performance. Finally, we can refer to value when customers associate the value of a purchase with an outcome they would like to achieve.

These measures of value are quite different from those deployed by most companies for evaluating the value of their business.

Accountants have suggested a panoply of measures (recorded value, assessed value, earning potential, etc.) that reflect their own conception of business and business logic. Economists offer much the same in proposing notions of use value, exchange value or cost value that correspond to their views of economic units and market mechanics. Purchasing and materials management offer yet another set of metrics (stock value, esteem value or replacement value) that are closely tied to theories on stock management and logistics.

Accounting and Finance	Economists	Purchasing and Materials Management	Consumers
Recorded value	Use value	Replacement value	Attribute-based value
Assessed value	Exchange value	Esteem value	Consequence-based value
Earning potential	Cost value	Stock value	Goal-based value
Liquidation value			

Figure 1.3 Client value
Source: Adapted from Wilson and Jantrania (1994)

There is no best way of measuring value, but there are metrics that have been designed to measure how business value is created and enhanced. Managers, in recognizing the importance of 'intangibles', are increasingly adopting non-traditional methodologies of measurement. Current approaches include the Balanced Scorecard, Economic Value Added, Total Cost of Ownership, and Value-based Management.[2]

Consider how the 'efficiency' paradigm of bigger, faster, better has conditioned the way managers look at business and business value. Process-centric applications have focused management's attention on organization and technology rather than people. Organizational culture, individual and team competencies and the quality of human relationships have taken a back seat while driving down cost is the predominant aim. In many cases, strategic decision-making has been performed using spreadsheets and process diagrams rather than observing how people and markets actually work. Taken to the extreme, as with the examples of WorldCom and Enron, the paradigm has even distorted the reasons why, and how, we do business.

Can information technology be designed to offer a different vision of reality? Can we design information architectures that will help management focus on factors other than cost and time, on the quality of interaction rather than the quantity of transactions, and on human motivation and innovation as the primary source of sustainable competitive advantage? This vision will require the introduction of a new paradigm of business value, new metrics for measuring 'better', and new models for structuring how we interpret data on our products, companies and markets.

What Are the Ingredients of Value?

Different client conceptions of exactly what constitutes value lead to conflicting visions of business value. As a result, information technology's measurable impact on the organization depends upon which elements or components of value we take into account. These elements include the following.

Efficiency

Efficiency can be seen as an input/output ratio that addresses the question of how work is being done today and what can be done tomorrow. Measuring efficiency involves capturing transaction costs of how people and/or technologies perform in a given process. Process-centric application systems, such as enterprise resource planning suites, focus our attention on the costs involved in managing key processes.

Profitability

Profitability measures the added value of an organization in comparing the cost of its resources with that of its products and/or services. Financial performance is usually equated with business success. The related concept of budgetability allows financial measurement of interdependent organizational units: cost centres, government departments or internal services. Measures of profitability usually form the nucleus of decision-making software packages.

Utilization

Utilization focuses on the extent to which company resources are employed at any given time. Measuring utilization involves evaluating how people, machines and materials are used in the production process. Stock management systems, for example, are often used not only to measure resource allocation, but also to suggest optimal uses of physical resources.

Quality

Quality has been defined variously as 'conformance to standards' and as 'conformance to expectations'. A common characteristic of quality measures is the evaluation of organizational products and services against external norms, legislation or objectives. Since these are basically benchmarking techniques, they can be easily adapted to measuring value in supply chains, markets or industries. Client relationship management software, to take one example, has been built on the premise that we can measure quality.

Innovation

Innovation can be understood in the context of an organization's ability to react to real or perceived changes in the market or in the economy. Although it is a response, reactive or proactive, to the current state of affairs, it is a measure more of potential than of past performance. Current applications of information technology are often ill-designed to measure innovation, because they focus both on the past (rather than the future) and on norms (rather than exceptions).

Passion

Passion represents the affective response of people to their work environment. Perhaps the most difficult of all measurements, passion is concerned less with conformance to requirements than with alignment of personal and professional expectations. Variables that influence passion include client perceptions of the workplace and work culture. Most implementations of information technology have failed to capture measures of passion, but have contributed directly to a decrease in company culture, individual passion and investment in the organization.

Knowledge

Knowledge is the lens through which employees apply, translate and create meaning out of the masses of data and information available to them. It can be viewed as a cultural ingredient, something that contributes to the feel of an organization, its climate and its atmosphere, and hence something that is tangible enough to be felt, experienced or transferred through to the customer. Surrogate measures may include the transparency of decision-making, levels of involvement, number of mistakes made and the ability to challenge conventional wisdom. Knowledge management systems have been designed around the premise that we can capture and communicate knowledge.

Effectiveness

Effectiveness can be viewed as an output–input ratio that addresses the question of 'doing the right things' to meet customer needs and objectives. Effectiveness measures the added value of an organization in adapting its product or service offer to the evolution of its clients' needs. Effectiveness is an evaluation of how people, rather than processes or markets, react to client demands. The inability of process-centric applications to capture or improve effectiveness has led to an increasing demand for collaborative technologies.

Box 1.1: Has the efficiency paradigm run out of steam?

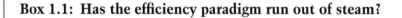

A vice-president of one of the world's leading software houses explained his business challenge in drawing two parallel lines on the board. He described his company as one of the most efficient on the planet: so efficient that most companies had already purchased their software. His challenge: convincing his sales managers that there was something else to sell. He pointed to the 'bottom line' and lamented that his sales force knew its importance only too well. He pointed to the top line and continued: how can you convince sales managers who have been bred on reducing costs to sell innovation, creativity and passion as a means of helping their clients apply information technology to build business value? He concluded that the efficiency paradigm had run out of steam, and that new measures of business value would be needed to fuel vision in the economy in the years to come.

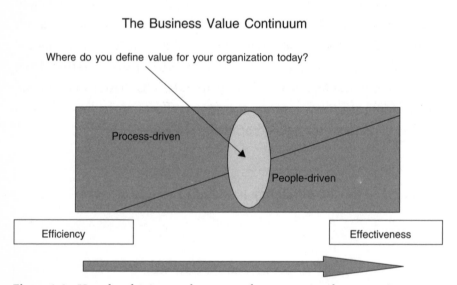

The Business Value Continuum

Where do you define value for your organization today?

Process-driven

People-driven

Efficiency

Effectiveness

Figure 1.4 How does business value emerge from operational processes?

Operational definitions of each value component vary from firm to firm depending on the company culture, the organization and individual beliefs. Since value is embedded in client relationships rather than products or services, it is by nature dynamic and subject to different interpretations over time. Specific value propositions are reflected differently on a continuum of organizational activities, from wholly automated tasks to intensively human-based processes. As a result, the foundations of business value are different for each organization, and reflect contrasting cultures and perspectives.

Different organizations in different industries at different stages in their development will be uniquely positioned on a business value continuum based on the nature of organizational processes, the proposed products or services, and how clients measure their value propositions. Attempts to build a stronger foundation for business value must begin by forging a common vision, and shared meaning, of how business value is defined within the organization. Information technology's ability to measure and to impact value does not depend uniquely on technology itself but on the coherence of what we are trying to improve.

Has Information Technology Played a Role in Building Business Value?

Several observers have questioned, over the years, whether information technology has played a direct role in creating business value. Strassmann, one of the most visible observers of the 'productivity paradox', argued steadily that, over the previous 10 years, 'there has been no relationship between the costs of information technology and profitability' (Strassmann, 1999). Joyce and Nohria (2003) concluded, having studied the performance of 160 companies over five years, that investments in information technology have little, if any, impact on corporate performance. They argue, using the criterion of total return to shareholders as a measure of performance, that management practices (including strategy, execution, culture, organization and, to a lesser extent, talent, leadership, innovation and M&A) are much stronger indicators of why certain companies outperform others.

Do IT investments in themselves produce a competitive edge? In the year 2000, nearly half of US corporate capital spending was used for information technology. Carr, in the recent, controversial *Harvard Business Review* contribution argues forcefully that 'IT doesn't matter' (Carr, 2003).[3] His argument suggests that information technology, like the railway and the electric generator before them, have become nothing more than commodity inputs. Carr categorizes IT today as an infrastructural technology that is easily acquired and copied, and proposes that IT's influence will henceforth be macroeconomic and not a means of competitive differentiation. Moreover, he believes that the IT market is saturated, since existing IT capabilities are largely sufficient for corporate needs. He concludes that the risks associated with implementing new information technologies exceed potential advantages, and that management should focus on securing their current investments and controlling costs.

As many have been quick to point out, IT alone does not create business value, but using information technology to support business strategy does.[4] Competitive advantage is not the result of computers but of skilled and innovative people who use information technology to implement efficient and effective business practices. Most consulting companies today suggest that information strategy can help improve business strategy along one of three dimensions: in improving the organizational knowledge of client needs and objectives (customer relationship management), in optimizing the delivery of products or services (supply chain management), or in increasing the visibility of the costs and benefits of organizational activities (enterprise resource planning). The logic behind each firm's business model helps determine which course of action will provide the greatest benefits for the organization.

The role of information technology today has greatly evolved from the simple calculating machine of the 1940s. Information technology can help management and employees better structure the demand for and the supply of, or better appreciate, the metrics with which value is measured. The role of many IT vendors has also evolved significantly, from simply shipping commodities to providing information services to business to decrease the risks of failure while increasing innovative uses of technology in the search for business value. The resulting value propositions can in turn be evaluated on several fronts: performance (will the vendor's proposal increase financial returns?), organizational design (does the operation improve the underlying technological infrastructure?), and/or the delivery of services (will the proposal improve company operations?).

Box 1.2: Dinner stories

As often happens when dining with clients after a business presentation, the conversation turned to particular points that David had raised earlier in the day. As a Senior Director for Market Development in a multinational corporation, he felt quite at ease exploring points of agreement and various differences of opinion, and punctuated the conversation with a number of anecdotes and stories. He felt somewhat more challenged when the client requested a hard copy of the presentation to work on in his hotel room later in the evening. It was not that he did not appreciate the attention, but neither he nor his client had a PC or printer at hand to reproduce the presentation ...

The conversation dimmed as David searched for an answer. He thought back to his work with the British schools on developing skills in information and communications technologies. He reviewed his own company's work on convergence: bringing the divergent digital technologies together into an integrated work environment. An instant before ordering dessert he proposed that the answer was only two phone calls away. He used his mobile phone to ask the client's hotel for its fax number. He then used the collaboration software on his phone to access a copy of the presentation on one of the company's servers, and to print it to the hotel fax machine along with a cover note. David had another story to tell, even before the coffee was cold!

Can We Propose a Roadmap for Business Value?

Improving business value can be undertaken through developing skills and competencies, improving organizational processes, and/or enhancing the technological infrastructure that supports a firm's product and/or service offer. Mistakenly, many firms attempt to work in all directions at once, more out of concerns that 'everyone's doing it' than as a result of their organizational strategy. Even worse, it is common to find contradictory initiatives between departments and between subsidiaries competing for a company's limited financial and human resources. Charting the proper roadmap for business improvement depends upon management's deeply rooted beliefs about where the value in their organization resides. Three fundamental questions correspond to three distinct dimensions of the Business Value Matrix™:

- Is the competitive advantage of your enterprise built upon a belief in superior talent, superior organization or superior technology?
- Will you best increase your competitive position in investing on an individual level (with certain managers, employees, business contacts), on a team level (by improving your sales or project team, or on a market level (in focusing on the relationships between your firm and its market)?
- To what degree do you measure success in improving the efficiency of business transactions (time and cost), and to what degree does success depend upon the effectiveness (quality, longevity, fidelity) of the interactions between your firm and its clients?

In crafting strategy based on management's deeply rooted beliefs about the sources of a company's value proposition, you inherently increase the chances of success.

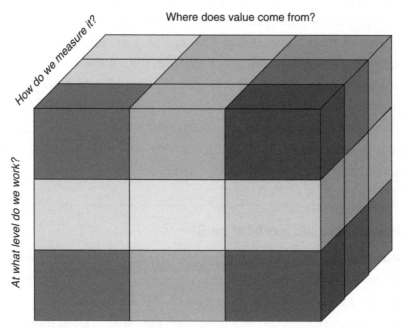

Figure 1.5 Where does value come from?

Where Does Value Come From?

Certain firms build their competitive position upon the strengths of their human resources: the quality of their managers, employees and/or business partners. These firms openly recruit and reward managers and employees who rise above the pack, and openly encourage creativity, innovation and initiative. Management will buy into proposals for process improvement or integrating new technology only to the extent that they improve their workforce's skills and competencies. In such a mindset, the roadmap to business value should focus primarily on how organizational and technological initiatives improve their human resources.

Other firms base their value proposition not so much on the quality of their human resources as on perceptions of an optimal organization of their human and physical capital. They believe that success resides in an organization of their processes and procedures that is 'better' than that of their competition. The roadmap for improving business value is fundamentally different here from that of those firms seeking to integrate the 'best and the brightest'; they should focus on how their managers and employees can use information technology to improve the organization's efficiency and/or effectiveness. The goal here is to improve the underlying business processes rather than the skills or competencies of their employees.

Box 1.3: We put our label on it!

Pedro, as the European Director for Strategic Investments of one of the world's major computer companies, had been invited to be the keynote speaker in a French MBA's workshop on the Information Economy. He began his talk with a description of

---

the long journey of his company from its incorporation as a computing, tabulating and recording company in 1911 to the Internet today. He paid considerable attention to an analysis of corporate strategy that had shifted from a focus on products to an emphasis on services and value. Before taking questions, he proudly showed the students what he considered to be his company's most innovative product.

It appeared to be similar to most other PDAs on the market: same size, same design, same programs and even the same components. The students' first question was how could he be so proud of a product that was certainly invented by a competitor, and that was neither revolutionary nor unique? He readily concurred, suggesting that the whole product was subcontracted from the initial requirement studies to after-sales service. Pedro concluded that the only thing his company produced for the product was the label, which was why the product had been sold successfully for 50% more than its competition.

Finally, some firms base their value proposition essentially on the quality of the tools that they put at the disposition of the organization. The underlying vision here suggests that value will come from putting the right tools in the right hands at the right time. Focusing organizational efforts on obtaining and deploying superior technology is seen as a source of competitive advantage. Although organizational strategies usually involve some combination of skill development, organization and technology, the effectiveness of the strategy will depend upon how companies view the source of their competitive advantage and where they believe their efforts will be most productive.

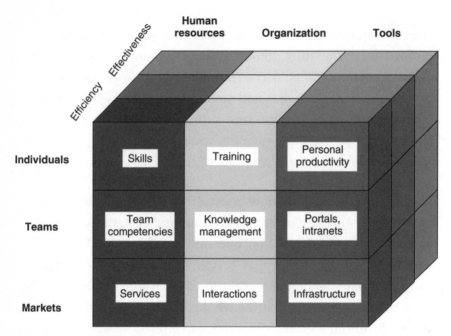

Figure 1.6 Strategies of business value

Where Do You Look for Value?

On a second dimension, the company can focus its efforts to build business value on individual managers, teams or departments, or the market as a whole. If the company's management believes that its value proposition is based on the quality of its individuals, business strategies should be deployed specifically to develop the individual's effectiveness in the organization. If the value proposition is based on people, this strategy suggests that efforts should focus on developing individual skills and competencies. On the other hand, if the goal is to optimize organizational processes, efforts at the individual level should be directed to perfecting training and education. Finally, if the company believes that its value proposition is technology-led, it could target its efforts at developing and maintaining personal productivity tools.

The view is quite different for firms that believe that the emphasis of building business value should be on developing the quality of its teams and departments. At this level, the company that wishes to favour human or social capital should focus on strategies that develop team skills and competencies.[5] This belief is founded on the premise it is not individuals' skills that add value to the organization, but their capacity to work as a team in addressing organizational challenges. Firms that privilege process over human capital will design knowledge management approaches that focus on organizational rather than individual learning. Firms that favour a technology-driven approach will develop portal strategies that provide the infrastructure to facilitate knowledge management and skill transfer throughout the organization.

It could be suggested that organizational strategy would best be served by firms focusing business strategies neither on their employees nor on their departments, but on the market itself. The belief here is that the market determines the value of a company's service offer, and therefore business strategies should attempt to develop knowledge of current and potential clients (prospects, business partners, government and regulatory agencies) likely to work with the company and the skills to deal with them. For firms focusing on people, this strategy would translate into efforts to improve the components of the company's service offer. If the company prefers an organizational approach, efforts would be directed at strengthening the processes that affect the quality of the interactions between the company and its external clients. Finally, firms that focus primarily on technology will begin by designing an information infrastructure that improves the company's impact in its markets.

How Do You Measure Business Value?

The third dimension of the Business Value Matrix™ concerns how each organization measures business value. As suggested previously, efficiency refers to transactional improvements in tasks, activities and processes. Improvements in efficiency are most often evaluated in terms of savings of time and/or cost. Conversely, effectiveness is about the degree to which human experience, innovation and knowledge constitute the foundations of business value. Effectiveness is more easily measured by a firm's external clients than by its technology, and is usually expressed as perceptions of quality, reliability and service.

Efficiency and effectiveness are not mutually exclusive, but constitute points on a continuum that includes profitability, innovation and passion. Both are necessary in building business value; the Business Value Matrix™ may be presented face up (or face down) depending on how each client views value. Nonetheless, the blend of value metrics should be adjusted to organizational beliefs concerning the source of business value and the level of intervention. Metrics can be constructed to measure the contribution of human resources, organization or technology to each organization's value propositions. Similarly, metrics can be captured at the individual, team or market levels consistently with where management feels value arises. The importance of specifying appropriate metrics is critical here, for they will influence how management evaluates market opportunities, measures business initiative, and communicates business value.

What Have We Learned?

Several conclusions can be drawn from this discussion. First we suggest that there is no one best way of using information technology to add value to business. Organizational strategies for business should be based upon the company's convictions about the source of its value proposition, as well as on what level it wishes to focus its efforts. Although there is clearly an interrelationship among a firm's skills, organization and technology, organizational strategy should be tailored to coincide with the particularities of each organization's culture and belief structure. Developing business strategies inconsistent with organizational culture, for example insisting on business process improvement in a company whose reputation has traditionally depended on the reputation of its managers, is unlikely to provide value.

In a similar vein, we suggest that improving business practice is not a 'packageable' solution but the core of business strategy. Organizational investments in information technologies will impact on, and be influenced by, investments in the key processes of the company. Just as importantly, the firm's IT infrastructure provides a great deal of information on the challenges of developing specific value propositions to improve business practice. The gaps or inconsistencies in information, the bottlenecks in delivering information to your clients, also indicate where and what employees, managers and business partners need to learn. Business strategies will benefit greatly from leveraging a company's current capabilities and future technology investments.

Notes

1. After obtaining the patent rights to a ball-pen created by Hungarian inventor, Ladislao Biro, Marcel Bich introduced his own ball-point pen in December 1950. As the world's number one manufacturer of ball-point pens, Bic today manufactures and sells 22 million stationery products every day around the world. See www.bicworld.com.
2. The notion of metrics will be explored in more detail in Chapter 3, 'Is What You Measure What You Get?'
3. Nicolas Carr develops his arguments, and presents a somewhat more balanced approach to the current debate in his book, *Does IT Matter?* (Carr, 2004).
4. See 'Does IT matter: An HBR debate', *Harvard Business Review*, June 2003.
5. Human capital refers to employees' practical knowledge, acquired skills and learned abilities that contribute to their productivity. Social capital offers a complementary notion in including the specific benefits that flow from the trust, reciprocity, information and cooperation associated with social networks. See Chapter 6, 'The Joined-up Economy'.

References

Carr, Nicolas G. (2003) IT doesn't matter (HBR OnPoint Enhanced Edition), 1 May 2003.

Carr, Nicolas G. (2004) *Does IT Matter?*, Boston, MA: Harvard Business School Press.

Deming, W. E. (1982) *Out of the Crisis*, Cambridge, MA: MIT Press.

Donovan, John, Richard Tully and Brent Wortman (1998) *The Value Enterprise: Strategies for Building a Value-Based Organization*, Toronto: McGraw-Hill Ryerson.

Drucker, Peter F. (1974) *Management*, London: Harper Row.

Joyce, William, and Nitin Nohria (2003) *What Really Works: The 4 + 2 Formula for Sustained Business Success*, London: HarperCollins.

Low, Jonathan, and Pam Cohen Kalafut (2002) *Invisible Advantage: How Intangibles Are Driving Business Performance*, Cambridge, MA: Perseus Publishing.

Schumpeter, Joseph A. (1934) *The Theory of Economic Development*, Cambridge, MA: Harvard University Press.

Scott Sink, D., and William T. Morris, with Cindy S. Johnstone (1995) *By What Method*, Atlanta, GA: American Institute of Industrial Engineers.

Strassmann, Paul A. (1999) *Information Productivity – Assessing the Information Management Costs of US Industrial Corporations*, New Canaan, CT: The Information Economics Press.

Wilson, D. T., and S. Jantrania (1994) Understanding the value of a relationship, *Asia–Australia Marketing Journal*, Vol. 1, 55–56.

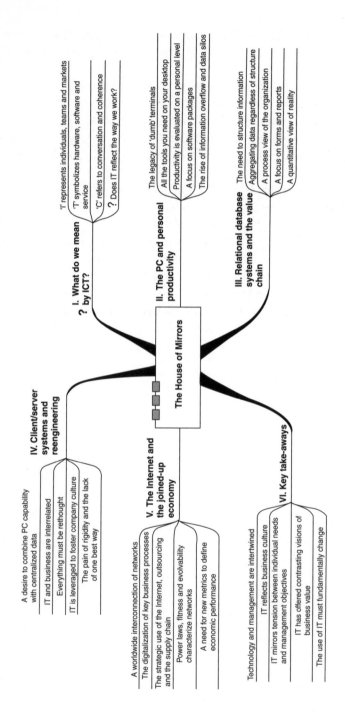

The House of Mirrors

I. What do we mean by ICT?
- 'I' represents individuals, teams and markets
- 'T' symbolizes hardware, software and service
- 'C' refers to conversation and coherence
- Does IT reflect the way we work?

II. The PC and personal productivity
- The legacy of 'dumb' terminals
- All the tools you need on your desktop
- Productivity is evaluated on a personal level
- A focus on software packages
- The rise of information overflow and data silos

III. Relational database systems and the value chain
- The need to structure information
- Aggregating data regardless of structure
- A process view of the organization
- A focus on forms and reports
- A quantitative view of reality

IV. Client/server systems and reengineering
- A desire to combine PC capability with centralized data
- IT and business are interrelated
- Everything must be rethought
- IT is leveraged to foster company culture
- The pain of rigidity and the lack of one best way

V. The Internet and the joined-up economy
- A worldwide interconnection of networks
- The digitalization of key business processes
- The strategic use of the Internet, outsourcing and the supply chain
- Power laws, fitness and evolvability characterize networks
- A need for new metrics to define economic performance

VI. Key take-aways
- Technology and management are intertwined
- IT reflects business culture
- IT mirrors tension between individual needs and management objectives
- IT has offered contrasting visions of business value
- The use of IT must fundamentally change

2
The House of Mirrors

*I*n the early 1990s, Alexandre, the owner of a textile manufacturing plant in the rural Ardèche region of south-eastern France
invited me to visit his firm. The visit began with lunch in the
lavishly appointed family dining-room set above the factory itself. In
the presence of his parents and children, the owner described in detail
the one hundred years of history and culture of the company, the
challenges of the European common market, and his hopes for IT. As
we enjoyed the several courses of the meal, he illustrated his story
by pointing through the room's bay windows to the frenetic pace
of the weaving machines, workflow and workgroups on the factory
floor below. After lunch, we first toured the production facilities and
then visited the computer room. The owner was as proud of his IT
investments as he was of his organization: three dedicated worksta-
tions – one for accounting, one for administration, and a third for
logistics...

Information and communications technologies – what is the proper
relationship between 'I', 'C' and 'T'? Let us assume that 'I' symbolizes individuals: people, teams and markets, and that 'T' represents
technologies, hardware, software and applications. 'C' would then
refer to the conversation or degree of coherence between the human
and technological visions of the world around us. As a whole, ICT
provides a more or less convincing reflection of our personalities and

our relationships with colleagues, managers and customers. If human vision and technological vision are aligned, ICT provides a lever for adding value to our jobs, our careers and our markets. If the two views are in conflict, ICT provides a source of anxiety, anger and persistent frustration.

Box 2.1: Information and communications technologies

Why are many employees openly hostile to information and communications technologies? The English sociologist, George Herbert Mead, defined the notions of 'I' and 'me' in relation to social experience: the 'I' represents our objectives, passions and vision, the 'me' is our understanding of how society sees us as individuals (Mead, 1913). In a similar fashion, we suggest that 'T' or technology is a mirror of the behaviour that management would like to reinforce. As an acronym, 'I' symbolizes individuals: people, teams and markets; 'T' represents technologies, hardware, software and applications; and 'C' refers to the conversation or degree of coherence between the human and technological visions of the world around us.

Does ICT today reflect the way you work, and the vision you have of your workplace? Since the conception of the first rudimentary computer in the 1930s, the deployment of successive generations of information technology has been justified as attempts to increase corporate productivity.[1] Although the link between the two has been hotly contested over the years, it is hard to deny that IT has influenced the way we think about producing more with less. Information technology, both as a lever for business value and a metaphor for how we structure business communities, has slowly been integrated into the heart of modern enterprise and into the core of management theory.

To better understand the interrelationship between technology and organization today, let us review their evolution over the last thirty years or so:

- How has information technology evolved over the last several decades?
- What are the characteristics of the successive generations of information technologies?
- How has technology influenced management practice?
- Have successive generations of technology required similar IT skills or significantly different approaches to levering IT for business value?
- Why has IT been so slowly adopted by the majority of the workforce several decades after its introduction in business?

The 'PC' and Personal Productivity

Since the conception of the first electronic calculating machines over half a century ago, the deployment of information technology has been justified by visions of increasing corporate productivity. Although the link between the two has been contested, it is hard to deny that IT has influenced the way we think about productivity. The evolution of information technology has impacted both the theory and the practice of management. To better understand this interrelationship between technology and organization today, let us quickly review some important business and technology milestones that have marked recent history.

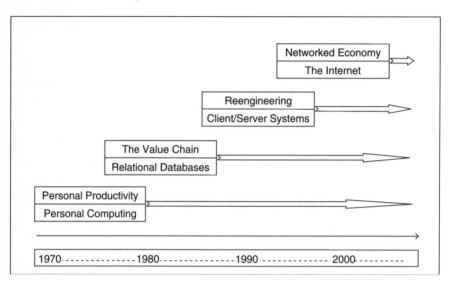

Figure 2.1   The recent evolution of information technology

Up until the 1970s, enterprise information systems were essentially built around central mainframes that contained the company's data and programs. End-users worked with 'dumb' terminals whose only functions were to capture and display the information stored on the mainframe. Centralized computer departments managed the system, controlling how, when and what information was available to each employee in the firm. Productivity, at least in relation to IT, was calculated for each firm by comparing results achieved with and without the use of comparable technology.

The introduction of the personal computer into business in the late 1970s was seen as a major technological innovation.[2] The innovation was not so much in its computing power as in its challenge to the existing paradigm of information management. Personal computers were able to store programs and data 'locally' and independently of the mainframe system. End-users had the possibility of organizing the information and installing the programs that they felt were the most useful in supporting their working environment. Many centralized computer services were ill-at-ease, if not openly hostile to their loss of visibility and loss of control of personal and departmental computing.

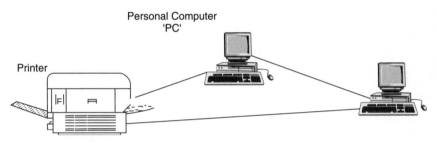

Figure 2.2 Personal computing

The era of *personal productivity* had dawned. Rather than being tied into the logic and the limits of the mainframe, PC users slowly but surely had all of the information tools necessary to work on their desktop. Without the chains of hierarchical control, employees and managers were 'freed' to become personally productive. The notion of IT 'productivity' changed as well: it was no longer seen as a strict synonym for quicker and faster, but could be equally associated with creativity and innovation. This technological evolution constituted a revolution in the practice of management: it defined productivity on a personal rather than an enterprise level; it shifted the emphasis from quantitative to qualitative aspects of doing business.

How have concepts of personal productivity shaped how we view work? To begin with, managers increasingly looked to computer departments, less for assistance in maintaining legacy systems than for help in exploiting the functionality of software packages. The end-user's vision of information technology shifted from communicating with highly centralized computer facilities to mastering desktop applications. Data was increasingly stored on the users' computers on floppy disks, hard drives and peripheral devices. Data was organized by application: text was associated with word-processing programs, data with spreadsheets, and graphics with presentation packages.

To what extent has the implementation of personal productivity software been a source of pain for employees, managers and customers (i.e. client pain)? Personal productivity software focuses the user's attention on software (word-processing, spreadsheet calculations and presentation graphics) rather than on the particularities of their business. Discussions with the computer department have focused more on functionality than on providing business value to internal or external clients. Storing data locally has often fostered both information overflow and data silos. Finally, the stored data ever more closely resembles the applications with which it was captured than the resources and transactions it was supposed to represent.

Relational Databases and the Value Chain

Information storage, indexing and retrieval have always been major challenges to enterprise. By the 1970s, it had become increasingly cost-effective for private companies to use the growing storage capability of computers to perform these tasks. Two main data models were developed to facilitate this task: IMS, which was based on hierarchical relationships, and CODASYL, which proposed network structures.[3] These models greatly simplified the organization of information concerning specific entities such as sales, marketing or logistics. Their major limitation was in comparing heterogeneous objects: it was impossible to compare sales receipts, marketing campaigns or stock without writing a complex program of pointer operations that would link the information together. Comparing these entities was as difficult in practice as in theory.

In 1979 a company called Relational Software, Inc. released Oracle, the first commercially available implementation of a relational database.[4] A relational database is a collection of data records in formally described tables from which data can be reassembled in many different forms without having to change the data's structure. As a consequence, data from sales, marketing and stock can be analysed together through simple requests or queries. From a technical point of view, it became possible for the first time to study sales, marketing and stock together to draw conclusions about their relative value to the firm.

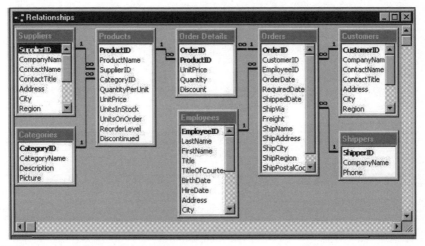

Figure 2.3   Relational database systems

Until some twenty years ago there was little theoretical justification to compare functions of the firm: productivity and value were attributes of the hierarchical organization as a whole. Comparing marketing and sales made no more sense than comparing apples with oranges until the notion of the *value chain* was introduced in management theory. In a hallmark publication in the early 1980s, Porter (1985) argued that the value chain implied that the contributions of specific functions of the firm could, and should, be analysed as they related to the primary and secondary activities of the firm.[5] The value chain is based on the process view of organizations as systems with inputs, transformation processes and outputs involving the acquisition and consumption of human and physical resources. How value chain activities are carried out determines costs and affects profits. Once again, an evolution in information systems coincided with a revolution in management theory.

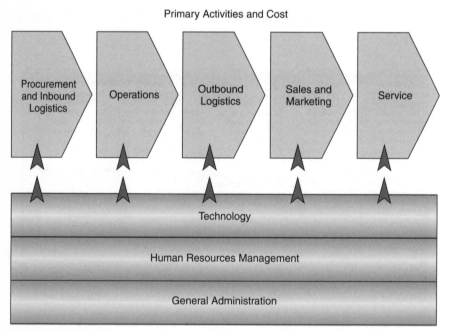

Figure 2.4 The value chain

How did concepts of relational databases shape how we viewed the organization of our business? To begin with, managers increasingly looked to computer departments for help in defining how to structure the data using models, tables and dictionaries. The end-user's vision of information technology shifted from creating isolated documents to producing forms and reports that could be used to share data across departments. Data for 'core applications' was increasingly stored on servers that were accessible across local networks rather than on isolated PCs. Multiple applications could run independently, each with its own data structures, logic and interface.

To what extent has the implementation of relational database software been a source of pain for employees, managers and customers? Structured relational databases focused the user's attention more on quantitative aspects of their business than on the softer 'data' of innovation, effectiveness and creativity. Discussions with the computer department focused more on normalizing data than on providing business value to external clients. The challenge of information overflow was actually intensified as the simplicity and power of these applications grew – users could save, and potentially analyse, seemingly limitless amounts of data.

Client/Server Systems and Reengineering

How should information be structured within a company? Before the introduction of the PC, this constituted a moot question: information systems were by definition hierarchical, consisting of dumb terminals connected to mainframe computers. The software written for mainframes was coded on a single level or tier; that is, the user interface, business logic (applications) and data were all contained in a single application. The adoption of the PC brought about the possibility of storing data and processing parts of applications on the user's desktop. The hierarchical nature of the information system was challenged by more horizontally distributed architectures.

By the 1990s a typical personal computer network required many specialized hardware devices and software packages to function. In addition, the languages and capabilities of databases were evolving and required more complex software, and more and more powerful computers to run them. Client/server architectures were introduced as a means to combine the capabilities of the newer PC applications with the benefits of centralized data. Client/server systems refer to architectures between two computer programs in which one program, the client, makes a service request to another program, the server, which fulfils the request. In a network composed of mainframes, applications servers and PCs, the client/server model provides a more coherent approach in interconnecting programs that are distributed efficiently across different departments within a firm.

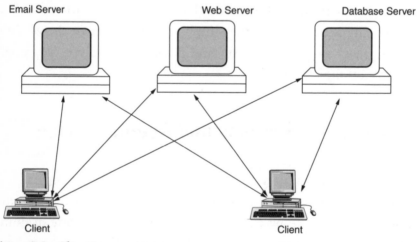

Figure 2.5 Client/server systems

How should activities be structured within a company? In 1990, Davenport and Short argued that improving business productivity required taking a broader view of how IT and business organization are interrelated. If hierarchical relationships no longer made sense in structuring information systems, could they not equally be questioned in the design of the organization itself? They argued the role of information technology was less in storing and retrieving information and more in fundamentally reshaping the way business is done (Davenport and Short, 1990). Michael Hammer and James Champy took the argument a step further in introducing the concept of reengineering: fundamentally rethinking and then radically redesigning business processes to achieve dramatic improvements in corporate performance.

Yet again, the evolution of information systems correlated with a revolution in management theory. As Hammer would write some years later,

> By bringing processes to the fore, reengineering turned organizations ninety degrees on their sides and caused managers to take a lateral, rather than a vertical, view of them. This shift has obviated the certainties and prescriptions of management textbooks. Virtually everything that has been learned in the twentieth century about enterprises applies only to task-centered enterprises, the hitherto dominant form of organizational life. For a world of process-centered organizations everything must be rethought: the kinds of work that people do, the jobs they hold, the skills they need, the ways in which their performance is measured and rewarded ....[6] (Hammer, 1996)

How have the concepts of reengineering and client/server systems shaped how we view our business? To begin with, managers increasingly looked to computer departments to design the infrastructure on which business will be shaped. Information technology, based on client/server systems, is often leveraged to instill and foster company culture. The end-user's vision of information technology has shifted from creating isolated documents to producing forms and reports that are used across business units. Data for 'core applications' is increasingly process-centric: horizontal models of best practice that cover core processes across departments, divisions and subsidiaries. Information technology has become an agent of transformation.

To what extent have process-centric applications become a source of client pain? Employees complain both of the excessive rigidity of this software, and the unwillingness of their software suppliers to adapt this technology to the particularities of their work environment. Managers worry that the adoption of such software will come at the expense of corporate culture and corporate identity. Some question the notion of 'best practice': Is there is one best way to organize firms regardless of size, industry and corporate vision? Finally, the substantial costs and time to get these systems up and running leave many worried about the real return on investment of such technology.

Box 2.2: Lean and leaner: the future of sensor technology

While radio frequency identification (RFID) technology has been around for years, it is increasingly gaining visibility as man-ufacturers and retail giants such as Wal-Mart, KiMs, Sernam and Metro Group are incorporating prototypes in their search for business value. All industries that work with tangible goods are potentially interested in this technology which provides near-real-time tracking without human interaction. As a result, a corporation can both optimize its supply chain and enrich its corporate assets with little labour cost. Improvements in the technology will make RFID economically practicable for large-scale deployments in the near future.

There is no doubt that sensor technologies – that translate phys-ical characteristics such as direction, temperature or pressure

---

into computer signals – have impressive potential for creating competitive advantage. Corporations will find that incorporating these technologies into their information infrastructure will allow them to create applications that monitor the real world rather than computer models, that respond to real-time data and not to forecasts and that capture information flows during a product's entire lifecycle. Business partners will be able to track assets more accurately, monitor key performance indicators and automate business processes, giving them greater insight into their operations and allowing them to make better decisions based on real-time information. Creating business value will nonetheless require more than just purchasing the technology; businesses will need to take better decisions to meet their clients' needs and objectives.

The Internet and the Joined-up Economy

How can information be communicated most effectively between organizations? In traditional information architectures, data was stored with the application on specific mainframes or servers. Specific programs were written to provide interfaces between data, logics and applications on the different servers within or between companies. These interfaces have been run in batches during non-peak hours to permit communication between sales, marketing, stock and accounting programs. The major handicaps of traditional architectures include the absence of real-time data exchange, the loss of data down to the lowest common denominator between programs, the difficulty in communicating the business logic between functions and firms, and the cost of maintaining multiple application-specific interfaces with different versions of software.

Box 2.3: Doing more with less

As information technology becomes an everyday commodity, IT developers and suppliers have tried to demonstrate that their products are capable of doing more for less. Increased competition and declining margins have led Oracle's CEO, Larry Ellison, to predict that in the near future 'Silicon Valley will more closely resemble Detroit', with just a few major actors and a number of small, specialized IT vendors. Oracle Corp. has thus focused its value proposition on grid computing: automating network administration and distributing more efficiently among groups of computers to lower the cost of ownership. IBM is privileging data warehousing and integration technologies to make it easier for clients to connect different databases. Microsoft Corp. continues to invest in the ease-of-use and interconnectivity of its applications and data analysis tools.

'More with less' directly addresses one of the major pains of most IT managers. As Gary Beach once lamented, 'less money to spend, less people on staff, less time to do it all' (Beach, 2003). IT managers have been forced to demonstrate that they and their staff are capable of doing more for less. They began by migrating their applications, from mainframes to minicomputers, then to PCs, local area networks and finally to the web. They have continued their efforts in outsourcing data management itself to supply chain partners and business partners via web services. Unfortunately, as IT becomes an everyday commodity, end-users produce greater amounts of data and line managers demand more concrete responses to their business challenges. 'More with less' perhaps can be better translated as a call to focus more on business value and less on technology as an end in itself.

The Internet constitutes a fourth wave of innovation in information systems. The Internet today is a worldwide interconnection of networks operated by government, industry, academia, and private parties with an agreement on communication protocols.[7] Although the origins of the Internet date back to the end of 1969, it began to be used widely in business at the beginning of this century.[8] One major characteristic of these networks is their three-tier architecture: the data, the applications and the user interface can be stored, indexed and retrieved independently of each other. As a result, information infrastructures can be distributed not only within a firm but within any business community. On many websites today, our enquiries for books, airline tickets and/or career guidance use interfaces, data and applications from multiple sources and locations.

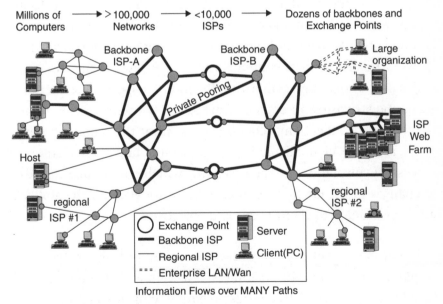

Figure 2.6 The Internet
Source: Russ Haynal, http://navigators.com/sessphys.html/.©navigators.com.

To what extent has this technological evolution influenced our thinking about management? The strategic use of the Internet, of outsourcing, and of the supply chain have led to concepts of the extended or networked enterprise. Characteristics of the networked economy include the digitalization of key business processes, the establishment of market standards for information exchange, the development of business communities around concerns of shared benefits, and the co-engineering of new market opportunities. As we will explore in Chapter 6, 'The Joined-up Economy', networked firms such as Cisco, e-Bay and Charles Schwab perform consistently better than traditional firms during periods of both economic growth and economic decline (Häcki and Lighton, 2001).

Barbasi takes these arguments several steps further in proposing his vision of the power of networks in the modern economy (Barbasi, 2002). He contends that our current distinctions between departments, firms and the market cloud a more valid vision of the economy around network nodes and their corresponding links. Borrowing from network theory, Barbasi contends that power laws, rather than normal distributions, determine the direction, scope and resilience of economic structures in emerging markets.[9] 'Fitness', or the number of links that connect any economic actor from the economic nodes, offers a degree of predictability in understanding their chances of success. 'Evolvability', or the ease with which core structures adapt to changes in the environment, correlate strongly with the ability of markets to adapt to client needs and objectives.

To what extent will the networked economy provide challenges to employees, managers and customers? To begin with, the relationship-based nature of networks contrasts sharply with the relatively static, relatively well-structured definitions of formal company structures. The management prescriptions of one best way, command and

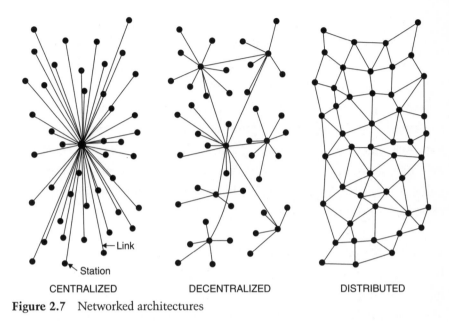

CENTRALIZED   DECENTRALIZED   DISTRIBUTED

Figure 2.7   Networked architectures

control, inherent in traditional management practice, may well prove ineffective or even counterproductive in channelling the influence and passion of social networks. The presence of dual structures of power, formal organizations and informal shadow networks will require new forms of governance within the firm, business communities and markets. Finally, new metrics for defining economic performance will challenge the efficiency paradigm of quicker and cheaper.

What Have We Learned?

Several conclusions can be drawn from this discussion. Technology and management are inherently intertwined: they cannot be analysed, implemented or optimized in isolation. In the context of business, information technology and management practice reflect company culture, vision and the prevailing cornerstones of management theory.

This observation goes a long way towards explaining why the introduction of information technology is often a source of intense anxiety for employees and managers alike. ICT can be seen as an acronym for how 'Individuals See Technology', as management's attempt to enhance or minimize human resources. This view of the value of information technology can contrast sharply with the employee's passions, needs and objectives. Introducing new versions of technology, or enhancing product features, does not contribute to business value if it conflicts with people's basic assumptions about the reality of work and the workplace.

The evolution of information technology in the last thirty years or so has closely mirrored that of management prescriptions for improving business practice. As if it took place in a house of mirrors, the introduction of PCs, relational databases, client/server systems and the Internet has offered contrasting definitions of where a business should focus its value propositions. These different approaches to structuring information systems have impacted how we define and measure business value. Succeeding generations of information technology, based on concepts of personal productivity, the value chain, reengineering and the networked economy, have introduced different and sometimes contradictory demands on what individuals need to learn to survive, to compete and to prosper in a business environment. The potential tension between individual needs and objectives and those reflected by each generation of information technology can help us understand why information technology has not led to greater increases in productivity.

Notes

1. The Atanasoff-Berry Computer has been considered the world's first electronic digital computer. It was built by John Vincent Atanasoff and

Clifford Berry at Iowa State University during 1937–42. It incorporated several major innovations in computing, including the use of binary arithmetic, regenerative memory, parallel processing, and separation of memory and computing functions. See http://www.cs.iastate.edu/jva/jva-archive.shtml.

2. The notion of a personal computer is attributed to Alan Kay, co-founder of the Palo Alto Research Center (PARC) in the late 1960s. Several years before the introduction of the Mac and the first PC, this missionary dreamed of 'a machine small enough to tuck under the arm'.

3. IMS, or Information Management System, began as a hierarchical database designed by IBM for Rockwell for the Apollo space program. It was used to track the bill of materials for the Saturn V. CODASYL, or Conference On DAta SYstems Languages, was in reality a volunteer organization formed in 1959 to guide the development of a standard programming language that could be used on many computers. This effort led to the development of COBOL.

4. The theoretical foundation for relational databases was formulated by Dr Edgar (Ted) Codd and published in 1969: *A Relational Model of Data for Large Shared Data Banks*. Ingres, from the University of California at Berkeley, provided the first academic initiative to pick up Codd's published work. Oracle was the first commercial product based on this work. Relational Software later came to be known as Oracle Corporation.

5. Most organizations engage in hundreds, and most often thousands, of tasks in the process of converting inputs to outputs. These activities can be classified generally as either primary or support activities that all businesses must undertake in some form. According to Porter (1985), the primary activities are inbound logistics, operations, outbound logistics, marketing and sales, and service. Secondary activities are procurement, human resource management, technological development and infrastructure.

6. Michael Hammer has since acknowledged that an overemphasis on process can lead to overlooking the vital role of people and practice (the way people actually work). He concludes that both are essential in improving business practice. See 'Process makes practice better', *CIO Magazine*, March 1 (http://www.cio.com/archive/030100_reply.html).

7. American National Standard for Telecommunications, Telecom Glossary, 2000, http://www.atis.org/tg2k/.

8. The origins of the Internet were in a project of the US Department of Defense – ARPANET – at the height of the Cold War that established four

nodes of computer-to-computer communication between the University of California Santa Barbara, UCLA, SRI International and the University of Utah.

9. Power laws refer to the concept of psychophysics that the magnitude of a subjective sensation, rather than adhering to a statistical normal distribution, increases proportionally to a power of the intensity of the stimulus.

References

Barbasi, Albert-Laslo (2002) *Linked: The New Science of Networks*, Cambridge, MA: Perseus Publishing.

Beach, Gary (2003) Doing more with less has limits, *CIO Magazine*, 1 December.

Davenport, Thomas H., and James E. Short (1990) Engineering: information technology and business process redesign, *Sloan Management Review*, Summer.

Häcki, Remo, and Julian Lighton (2001) The future of the networked company, *The McKinsey Quarterly*, Number 3.

Hammer, M. (1996) *Beyond Reengineering*, New York: Harper Business, pp. xi–xiii.

Mead, George Herbert (1913) The social self, *Journal of Philosophy, Psychology, and Scientific Methods*, Vol. 10, 374–380.

Porter, Michael (1985) *Competitive Advantage: Creating and Sustaining Superior Performance*, New York, The Free Press.

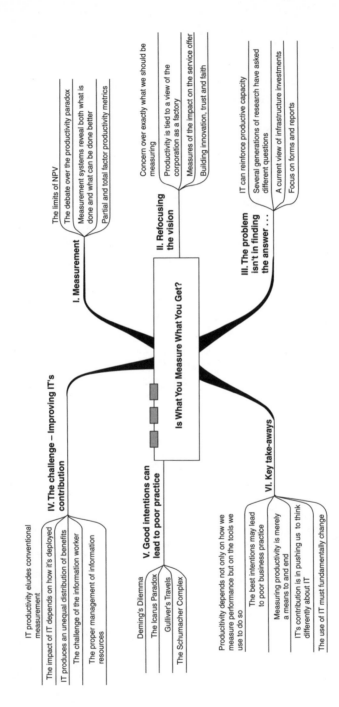

3
Is What You Measure What You Get?

*T*wo years ago, I had the pleasure of discussing business with Sean, the Director of Sales of the leading IT supplier at that time in Ireland. The pleasure was tarnished with a tint of regret, since this jovial, stout and balding Irishman was soon to leave the company that had employed him for the last twenty years. He strongly disagreed with his managers in the USA over the importance of the variable expenses that were associated with his sales success. His management, citing the figures from the newly installed ERP system, accused his team of spending significantly more than the company average on client entertainment. He did not contest the figures, but argued that corporate sales in Ireland had more to do with face-to-face conversations than virtual communication through the Internet. Today, Sean is comfortably retired and remains a contributor to evening conversations in the local pubs. His former company, having adopted best practices of Internet sales, has seen their client base plummet.

In this chapter we will explore how information technology has been deployed to measure business value. We will argue that 'productivity' depends not only on how we measure performance but on the information technology we use to do so. Importantly, the value proposition of information technology on performance reaches far beyond what we are currently capable of measuring. What you measure is not necessarily what you get: we will explore how good intentions concerning information technology can lead to poor business practice. We will conclude that the most significant contribution of information technology is not its ability to precisely measure value, but its capacity to push us to think differently about the relationship between what we measure and how we wish to improve our business.

Most accountants will readily argue that the value of information technology depends upon financial calculations of net present value or the internal rate of return. They suggest that these metrics can be calculated in comparing the cost of the investment (weighted by the hurdle rate) with the expected IT and business benefits. Unfortunately most accountants, and information technology specialists for that matter, are at a loss to explain how to accurately gauge the notion of benefits. The weight of cumulative benefits, or those that impact several parts of the business, have proved extremely difficult to capture with traditional accounting methods. Should the definition of benefits be restricted to the improvement of your organization's information infrastructure, or extended to improvements in what your company offers to your managers, business partners and clients? How do investments in information technology improve corporate productivity, and which metrics best demonstrate the added business value?

To better understand how investments in information technology affect corporate productivity, we will explore a number of questions:

- If information technology helps us be 'quicker, faster and better', why are we not more productive?

- What should information technology be measuring?
- Does IT in itself contribute to productivity?
- What are the dangers of how IT currently measures value?
- How can we improve our use of value metrics?

Box 3.1: What drives value?

In the wake of the Enron crisis, Louis Thompson, CEO of the National Investor Relations Institute, asked the Securities and Exchange Commission roundtable, 'When company officials sit down with the institutional investors and have a discussion about the business, the kinds of things that you're talking about – what drives value? What are the value drivers? What are the critical things that management is most concerned about? – a lot of times that discussion goes into the realm of intangible assets and nonfinancial information' (SEC, 2002).

Louis went on to relay the claim of Professor Baruk Lev that five out of every six dollars of market value of our largest corporations cannot be found in the financials. If financial metrics do not account for business value, other measurement criteria do help explain why certain companies are valued more highly than others. According to Lev's research at the Stern School, these intangibles include how organizations structure opportunities to develop innovation, talent and communities of practice with their business partners and customers. Financial metrics may be easier to analyse, but they have proved to be very poor indicators of a company's perceived value.

How Do You Measure Productivity?

Do investments in information technology actually improve corporate productivity? As early as July 1987, the Nobel Prize-winning economist Robert Solow commented, 'We see the computer age everywhere except in the productivity statistics' (Solow, 1987). This conclusion has given birth to two decades of debate over the reality of the so-called *productivity paradox* (see Diewert and Fox, 1999). Concern over the impact of information technology on performance persists, leading Nicolas Carr to conclude recently, 'Studies of corporate IT spending consistently show that greater expenditures rarely translate into superior financial results. In fact, the opposite is usually true' (Carr, 2004).

In our view, the productivity paradox is essentially a result of the use of information technology both as a measurement tool and as a source of corporate performance. We have argued previously that the nature of business value has changed significantly over the last few decades. Business value is a result of a number of factors of production, as well as of the corporate vision of where the organization has been and where it would like to go. The ability of information technology to measure business value depends upon how clearly these factors are defined, aggregated and communicated throughout the organization.

Measurement systems reveal both what is actually produced within an organization and what can be done better. In developing operational measures of business value, management provides the link between corporate vision and reality. Measures of business value are designed to promote three objectives: to raise awareness about what business value means to the organization, to establish guidelines for understanding the relationships between business value, performance and productivity, and to identify a learning agenda to heighten the business value of future products and services.

Information systems are designed to measure specific aspects of productivity; they attempt to capture its different or complementary facets, or to deduce future scenarios from past performance. Based on the typology provided by Parsons, we can distinguish between partial and total factor productivity measures (Parsons, 2002). Partial productivity metrics are probably the most commonly implemented technique. They are frequently designed to offer insight into labour, materials or capital productivity. Labour productivity – output divided by the labour input – is the easiest to measure. It is measured as the value of output divided by either the hours of labour used in the production of a good or service, or the average employment of human resources in a given period.

Capital productivity, in which output is divided by total capital input, complicates measurement significantly. This is because it is much more difficult to define a physical unit of capital than it is for labour. It is also more challenging to accurately measure the amount of capital actually used up in producing a fixed term of output. Traditionally, these productivity metrics capture ratios such as *customers serviced per bank teller, fabric produced per loom, contracts signed per sales representative*. Spreadsheets, databases, accounting or sales systems have widely applied formulas similar to those in Table 3.1.

Table 3.1 Productivity measurements

Measurement	Formula	Typical industry
Capital productivity	Units sold/m^2 floor space	Retail
Energy productivity	Miles travelled/fuel used	Trucking
Labour productivity	Courses taught/teacher	Education
Materials productivity	Chocolate produced/kg cocoa	Food processing

Source: Adapted from Parsons (2000).

What partial metrics gain in simplicity, they often lose in analytical scope. It is difficult to accurately account for all of the variables that impact capital, energy and/or labour. It is often misleading to isolate one type of productivity from another: labour influences capital productivity and vice versa. Finally, although these metrics shed some light on past performance, they are very poor indicators of future performance.

Total factor productivity metrics are calculated most often as a measure of value added rather than productivity. Total factor productivity metrics seek to compare the total output of an organizational unit (activity, firm, supply chain) with the resources used to generate that output (Brynjolfsson, 1993). These measures are essentially benchmarking techniques. They can be designed to measure current performance with performance in a similar time period in the past or in the future. They can also be constructed to compare the organizational unit with other units within the same organization or across the industry.

Total factor productivity metrics help to define what can be considered 'acceptable performance' in terms of budget, cost, return on investment or quality. They are generally considered more reliable than partial indicators in predicting future economic performance. They are extremely difficult to elaborate, analyse and communicate effectively without relying on information technologies. These metrics form the basis of modern financial and accounting techniques, including productivity accounting, activity-based costing and EVA (economic value added) which are outlined in what follows.

Table 3.2 Total factor productivity

Measurement	Formula	Typical use
Total productivity outputs	Gross output − (Labour + Capital + Materials + Energy)	Financial forecasting Market analysis

These traditional methodologies of measuring IT productivity are closely tied to the mindset of the workplace as a type of factory that transformed physical goods into measurable products (Davis *et al.*, 1993). One of the difficulties faced by the measurement techniques is that many modern enterprises do not directly manufacture much at all; they depend upon a growing network of subcontractors and business partners to produce the components and products that they brand, sell and eventually service. Productivity depends not only on how we measure performance but on how we use information technology to do so.

Attempts to associate investments in IT with increases in corporate productivity may prove to be more of an illusion than a paradox. Manufacturing industries, which over the last century have contributed to productivity gains of nearly 5% per annum, account today for less than 25% of the workforce. Knowledge and service industries, in which productivity 'gains' have been markedly slower, now account for nearly 75% of the workforce. Is the drop in productivity statistics due to the nature of industry itself, or to the inability of traditional measurement techniques to take into account the newer forms of performance?

Box 3.2: Keep the change

Thomas Cook is one of the longest-serving and best-known brand names in the travel business. In the late 1990s the Travellers Cheques division embarked upon a series of initiatives to improve the efficiency of this time-tested activity. The financial model for Travellers Cheques is intricately tied to the process that it operates on huge volumes with tiny margins. Profits

---

depend upon the 'tail' of the activity: the number of cheques that have been issued and paid for but not encashed. Profits have been steadily declining industry-wide under tremendous pressure not only from the increased use of credit cards but from the introduction of the Euro.

Under the leadership of a well-known consulting firm, Arthur headed up a major process reengineering effort to identify appropriate metrics for improving the Travellers Cheques business. His project team of three spent six months organizing company workshops on this subject, and then analysing hundreds of potential measures: process metrics, customer satisfaction, capital expenditures, inputs, outputs, environmental concerns and a host of surrogates. At the end of the day they came to a consensus on one important conclusion: that the efforts were totally out of proportion with the foreseeable benefits. Designing appropriate metrics was not the problem, it was the effort needed to redesign the process to gather better information. Arthur concluded that most organizations are beautifully designed to get what they get. Improving the metrics will not impact performance unless the organization is willing to fundamentally change the way it goes about its business.

Another difficulty with these methodologies can be identified in the nature of productivity gains in the last two decades. Increases in industrial capacity during this time period pale in comparison with demonstrable improvements in service, quality and convenience. Nonetheless, the time-tested formula of substituting capital for labour and talent has proved to be less effective in service-based industries (Davis *et al.*, 1993). Does information technology reinforce dated views of the firm as a factory or can it be adapted to capture new visions of business value?

Productivity Accounting

Several methodologies have been tried to improve productivity measures by accounting for the changing reality of the organization. The goal of such efforts is to analyse an activity or organization's ability to create wealth (the top line) and not simply to keep the score of its current use of human and capital resources (the bottom line). As a result, a variety of techniques have been proposed to distinguish productivity from cost-effectiveness or price recovery.

Productivity accounting is particularly attractive in that it offers a direct link between the total productivity of the organization and its financial results. Hayzen and Reeve argue that this approach measures the change in total resource productivity and gauges the corresponding changes in business profitability (Hayzen and Reeve, 2000). It says how much wealth was created or destroyed by the organization and who, if any, were the beneficiaries. Productivity accounting is helpful in understanding notions of profit in the networked economy, in 'non-profit' sectors of the economy, or in commercial operations dominated by 'cost centres'.

Productivity accounting offers managers a clear set of benefits:

- Productivity changes can be quantified, allowing quantitative and qualitative trade-off analysis.
- Performance can be explained in relation to performance and profits.
- Changes in quality can be compared to variations in cost, revenues and profitability.

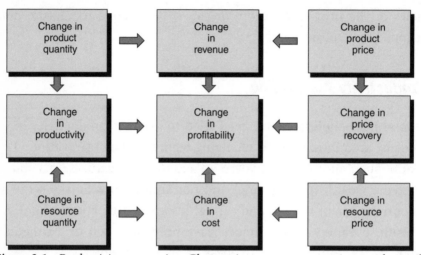

Figure 3.1 Productivity accounting. Changes in any one resource impact the availability or use of other resources

Source: Hayzen, A.J. and J.M. Reeve (2000) Examining the relationships in productivity accounting, *Management Accounting Quarterly* (Summer), 32–39.

- The role of accounting can be expanded from simple 'counting numbers' to contributing to business value.

Activity-based Costing

Activity-based costing (ABC), and similar concepts (activity-based management, transaction-based costing), are measurement methodologies that assign costs to activities rather than to products or services. This enables resources and overhead to be more accurately assigned to the products and the services that consume them. Although the consumption of direct resources can be easily traced to cost objects (materials and labour, for example), indirect costs such as supervision, information technology and human resource management must be similarly allocated using a predetermined set of procedures.

ABC involves measuring cost drivers (factors such as administration or utilities) whose variation will impact the relative weight of a cost object. Accountants can then estimate distinct indirect 'cost accumulation pools' for the cost objects that define a given activity. Each cost object may have one or several cost drivers. Process-centric information technologies, and notably enterprise resource planning packages, offer the scope and uniformity of analysis necessary to perform activity-based accounting.

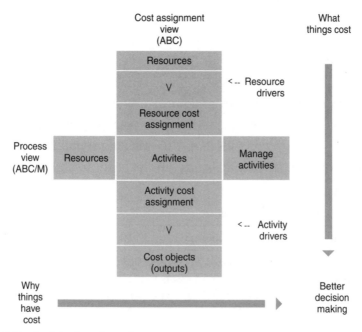

Figure 3.2 Activity-based costing
Source: The Activity Based Costing Portal, http://www.offtech.com.au/abc/Home.asp

Economic Value Added

Economic value added, or EVA, as well as similar approaches such as MVA, TSR and CFROI, has been developed to determine the value of corporations and investments.[1] The notion of EVA is that an organization creates business value only if the return on its capital exceeds the opportunity cost of acquiring the capital from lenders or shareholders who could have invested more profitably elsewhere. The underlying assumption of EVA is that productivity analysis must calculate and integrate the cost of capital as well as that of human and physical resources. EVA is calculated by deducting from the after-tax operating profit a charge on the amount of capital it employs.

The Economic Value Added (EVA) is thus a measure of surplus value created on an investment. This approach was developed by the American consulting firm, Stern Stewart. EVA focuses (through adjustments) primarily on cash flow, since the latter is much more difficult to manipulate than price recovery or short-term profits and is therefore a more reliable indicator of performance. Stern Stewart also claims that EVA provides an early warning signal insofar as EVA will often turn negative long before profits begin to show a decline.

Table 3.3 Economic value added

Measurement	Formula	Typical use
Economic value added	Capital invested in assets in place + PV of EVA from assets in place + Sum of PV of EVA from new projects	Micro- or macro-economics

Refocusing the Vision of IT Productivity

Since measurement systems are designed to capture what is actually produced within an organization, there can be legitimate concern over exactly what we should be measuring. If a firm's productivity today is not tied as closely to the quantity of physical products produced as it is to the quality of its product/service offer, productivity improvements should be measured differently. Information technology's impact on business performance can similarly be extended from simply measuring time and cost to evaluating effectiveness and performance. Refocusing on the nature of business value can go a long way towards resolving Solow's productivity paradox.

There are several methodologies for measuring IT's impact on business performance. These range from more traditional metrics of time and cost to various conceptions of quality based on product or service attributes, on consequences or on client objectives. This panorama of measurements forms the distinct axis of an IT value matrix ranging from efficiency to effectiveness. If no one measure is better than another, the measures together constitute different facets of business value. Understanding the interdependence of these measurements is crucial in coming to grips with the interdependence of IT and organizational performance.

As mentioned earlier, traditional measures of IT productivity are closely tied to a view of the corporation as a factory which essentially produces goods and services. In this view, the investments in IT should have a measurable impact on the cost and/or quantity of a firm's products. Recent history has demonstrated this point in industries where investments in IT have been the greatest – banking, leisure, entertainment. Information technology has undeniably improved the productivity of these sectors. Equating IT productivity with increases in productive capacity may prove to be more of an illusion than a paradox.

What are really required, of course, are operational measures of the impact of information technology on the quality of a firm's service offer. There has been considerable attention in management literature given to discussing measures of IT's impact on customer satisfaction, customer loyalty collaboration and service quality (Macdonald *et al.*, 2000). The authors suggest that IT's impact is not necessarily either within the activity or within a given process, but directly upon how the client discovers, engages and evaluates a company's value proposition. In this context IT productivity has less to do with productive capacity than it has with business value.

Another view of IT productivity is grounded in arguments of 'missed' opportunity costs. As Quinn and Baily (1994) explain, 'The managerial decision for IT infrastructures is generally not *whether* to invest, but rather how to obtain needed compatibilities at lowest cost ... several firms noted that the only truly rigorous way of evaluating many infrastructure payoffs would be to calculate the opportunity cost of "not being in that business"; i.e., the total business loss that would have been incurred if the investment had not been made'. The argument here is that if the benefits of investments in IT are difficult to gauge, the costs of not investing in information technology are plain for all to see.

A final view of IT's impact on productivity looks at its value in building innovation, trust and faith. The argument here is that the real value of information technology cannot be appreciated fully unless we take into account how these investments affect motivation in the workplace. McGehee (2001) argues this point eloquently in discussing the value of passion when distinguishing the use of IT in creative versus conformity companies. Handy (1995), and more recently Galford and Drapeau (2003), have stressed the potential role of information technology in building trust in organizations. This view is in sharp contrast to common perceptions of IT's role in dehumanizing the workplace. Perhaps the link between information technology and business value has less to do with how we use information technology than with the investment in technology itself.

The Problem Is Not in Finding the Answers, but in Asking the Right Questions

On one level, IT architectures are designed to capture data and information on what is produced by an organization. On another level, information technology can reinforce a firm's productive capacity; i.e. the measurement tool is also a lever of business value inside the firm and the business community. What exactly do we mean by IT productivity and how has this definition evolved over the years? Should IT's contribution be limited to how accurately it measures productivity and business value or extended to how it influences our definitions and search for business value?

We previously defined productivity as a ratio of inputs to outputs. IT productivity was thus associated with economies of manual effort: investments in information technology were thought to inevitably lead to reductions in the workforce. As Strassmann's research into the productivity paradox brought to light, there is little correlation between investments in IT and labour productivity (Strassmann, 1997).

A second wave of research has attempted to correlate IT investments with improvements in 'total factor' productivity. As previously defined, this term suggests that the costs of the IT infrastructure should be measured against a set of inputs including labour, capital and physical goods. Economists suggested that even if IT did not directly lead to reductions in the workforce, it would inevitably lead to economies in capital and physical investments. Unfortunately, research does not support this contention either: in spite of large absolute increases in corporate spending on IT infrastructure, the average growth in total factor productivity (labour productivity) fell from 3.25% in the 1960s to just 1.09% (1.81%) by 1992 (Brynjolfsson, 1993).

In the last decade industry observers began suggesting that linking IT investments to tangible indicators of productivity was perhaps missing an important point. IT experts argued that the Internet had been much more than a vehicle for communicating data; information technology had become a vehicle for creating business value. In sum, IT was viewed as an integral part of corporate strategy that rendered efforts to measure its productivity superfluous. Management theorists who insisted on measuring the return on IT investments struggled with the advice of practitioners such as Frederic Smith who warned of the futility of crunching numbers,

> My advice to them would be to (invest) .... they're going to be toast if they don't .... it's very disconcerting when you know you have to do it but you run your traditional analyses and can't find an ROI to meet demand. But you know that if you don't somebody else will, and you'll be in real trouble. (Smith, 1999)

Research on information technology shifted from analysing IT productivity to stressing its use in producing 'massive competitive advantage'. As Macdonald, Anderson and Kimbel have argued, although there are today a variety of empirical techniques for measuring IT investments, they simply are not used (Macdonald *et al.*, 2000).

In current literature, the desire to link IT investment and productivity has become less and less evident. IT investment is seen more and more to focus on measuring or managing information, and therefore cannot be expected to contribute directly to productivity. Carr suggests that IT investments should be assimilated with infrastructure investments such as telecommunications and transportation. In this light, expectations of direct productivity increase are unrealistic. For management research the IT paradox has taken on another dimension: beyond deciding how much IT impacts corporate performance, many are wondering whether the problem is not in finding the answer as much as it is in asking the right question.

What Can Be Done to Improve IT's Contribution to Corporate Performance?

The confusion over whether IT's contribution to business value is direct in its impact on business productivity or indirect in its ability to measure value is part of the explanation of the so-called productivity paradox. This aside, what other factors can explain why it is so difficult to measure IT's impact on business value? More importantly, what can be done to improve IT's contribution to corporate performance? To address the concerns about the return on IT investments, we need to come to grips with why firms have had so much trouble measuring IT's impact on the way we work. Concerns over appropriate metrics, timeframe and scope explain why IT productivity often eludes measurement by conventional approaches.

As originally pointed out by Brynjolfsson (1993), one of the major reasons for the 'IT productivity gap' is a lack of consensus over exactly what we should be measuring. How exactly does information technology impact performance? Companies introduce information technology for a variety of reasons: to ensure a better circulation of information, to improve individual and team competencies, to introduce new skills and processes, and eventually to build flexibility into the organization to better address market opportunities and challenges. The impact of information technology depends more on how it is applied within the organization than on what we are trying to improve.

A second difficulty in measuring the impact of IT concerns the timeframe in which we expect productivity improvements. The payback for using IT to facilitate a better circulation of information is quicker than that for using IT to encourage organizational flexibility. The return on investment may be just the opposite: if improving information flows is tactical, organizational agility constitutes a strategic goal. The more ambitious the organization's goals, the more time is needed for individual learning and adjustment. As a consequence, there is no unique timeframe in which to evaluate the return on IT investments.

Macdonald *et al.* point out yet another difficulty in that IT investments produce an unequal distribution of benefits. The introduction of information technology can potentially improve an isolated activity, the synchronization of activities, an entire process inside a firm, or eventually other processes within the business community. The improvement can provide a source of sustainable competitive advantage, contribute to product differentiation, or simply fulfil a condition for the firm to remain competitive in a given market. The example of the ATM in the banking industry is a case in point: investments in ATMs are no longer a source of profits or even product differentiation, but are a requirement to compete in retail banking.

A different challenge concerns dealing with the information worker. It is difficult to define the output or contribution made by the white-collar/knowledge worker. To begin with, white-collar/knowledge workers, unlike production workers, are often unaccustomed to being measured. It is necessary to specify the outputs, making clear distinctions between results and activities – being productive rather than just busy. Moreover, quantity and quality are often inseparable and the quality of the output is even more difficult to ascertain than the quantity. Finally, the distinction is not always made between efficiency and effectiveness and, in order to be productive, the white-collar/knowledge worker must be both efficient and effective.

A final difficulty arises from the 'proper' management of information resources. Information technology has traditionally been the responsibility of the IT department. IT managers were judged on their ability to distribute the resources as largely as possible within the firm, and to keep the systems up and running. In such a schema, line managers do not own IT, and 'consume' IT resources without considerations of cost or return on investment. Nevertheless, as perceptions of information technology evolve, IT ownership is gradually shifting both from distributing resources to providing service and from consuming resources to taking responsibility for IT management. Traditional measures of productivity struggle to take into account business ownership of IT: IT productivity is nothing more, and nothing less, than IT's contribution to your business.

Good Intentions Can Lead to Poor Business Practice

If debate has flourished around the potential impact of information technology on business value, there are also abundant examples of IT usage that actually diminishes or detracts from the manager's contribution to business value. If business value comes from human contributions in improving a company's product or service offer, individual or collective behaviour can also dilute or pollute a company's value proposition. Beyond ill-will or lack of competence, poorly applying information technology can potentially mislead employees, managers and clients alike into mental cul-de-sacs that endanger a firm's culture and mission. Let us quickly take a look at several of the more frequently travelled paths.

The first can be labelled *Deming's Dilemma*. The mantra 'what gets measured gets managed' is more relevant than ever in these days of management method, with the result that management attention is focused on what can be measured most easily and neglects what is less easy to measure. IT has allowed much performance to be quantified very easily – every finger tap at the supermarket checkout – but has trouble with the little qualitative things – the cashier's smile or kind words – that draws the customers' attention and gratitude. In an economy where value is a characteristic of relationships rather than products or even services, we can question whether what you measure is really what you get.

Box 3.3: Garbage time . . .

Sarah, the European Managing Director of an international pharmaceuticals company, was faced with quite a dilemma. Her Board of Directors in the USA had asked her to close down one of her subsidiaries on the basis of the production costs supplied by the corporation's enterprise resource planning system. Sarah indirectly oversaw the design and input of the data in Europe, and knew that the aggregate figures greatly misrepresented the reality. Her punctual checks of the data had revealed an error ratio approaching 50% at certain times for certain cost objects.

She later admitted that she was in quite a fix: either she admitted faults in the data administration under her responsibility, or she implemented a decision with high social costs based on faulty data. She did try suggesting in several memos and several conversations that other metrics could be taken into consideration. Her MBA education reminded her of the 'irrefutable' logic of ratios like NPV and IRR. After exploring the options with her closest

---

advisers, she opted to close down the subsidiary, respecting the company targets for efficiency.

The argument can be taken a step further to reach what Pinsonneault and Rivard called the *Icarus Paradox*. This explains the productivity paradox in terms of middle managers devoting more and more of their time to those activities – detailed reports, task forces and working late – that they hope will draw them closer to the organizational gods (the managing directors). In doing so they become increasingly specialized and neglect the traditional generalist strengths of the middle manager. Rather than become indispensable to top management, this transformation of managers into high-flying specialists leaves them vulnerable to the actual outsourcing of their activities in the drive towards organizational efficiency.

Box 3.4: Efficacy mail

In an e-mail entitled 'efficacy mail' sent to all the employees of his Dutch subsidiary, the local CFO of a multinational information services company publicly singled out his employees with the highest telecom bills. Using a well-known financial analysis package, the CFO drilled down to identify multiple criteria by employee: the total phone bill, highest international phone costs, ratio of international versus national calls, and calls from mobile phones. In his vision of the company's drive to lower operating costs, he strongly advised these employees to 'take the appropriate action'.

Andreas, one of the top culprits of this 'wall of shame', wearily responded in private to his management that perhaps what

---

you measure is not what you get. What significance do these figures have, he wondered, without taking into account the nature of each employee's activities, the corresponding savings in travel costs, the profitability of these transactions? How could an international information services company stay in touch with its clients, foster a climate of proximity and collaboration, without an extensive use of telecommunications? He concluded his message with a comment from one of his fellow-managers: perhaps the 'appropriate action' to take to get off this 'most wanted' list would be to go back to travelling five days a week.

Yet another source of concern can be dubbed *Gulliver's Travels*. This argument stems from observations like those of Carr (2003) that the competitive advantage of IT declines in proportion to its use in a market. IT's potential benefits, including increased productivity, are far from universal and are only effective if applied at the right level – individual, department, organization, sector – and for the right purpose. In other words, depending upon the specificities of the firm and its market, the goal of increasing productivity may be contested by client needs for quality or appearance. What can be seen as an effective lever of productivity at one level or in one instance can be seen as too little or too late from another point of view.

A final preoccupation is the *Schumacher Complex*. Managers may abandon attempts to achieve productivity gains in favour of new goals, such as greater market share or greater managerial control. For instance, the current movement towards new investments in client relationship management may in part be explained by the failure of organizations today to capture measurable benefits from their past IT investments. In the race for corporate performance 'winning' becomes an end in itself – an obsession that too often may even lead some managers to forget why they are competing in the first place. The radical change demanded by business process reengineering provides an excuse for any change in management strategy required for IT.

How Does IT Contribute to Productivity?

The presumption that investments in IT lead to productivity gains has become so commonly accepted that many managers seem to forget that measuring productivity is merely a means to an end and not an end in itself. Information technology becomes part of the way we structure the workplace. No matter which core process we examine, it is rare today not to find that at least parts of each business process are dependent upon information technology. One of the basic tools of business process improvement is the introduction of information technology to replace physical transactions (for example, optimizing stock management rather than increasing minimum levels of stock). In such a light, information technology can be seen to be an integral part of the process of how we work. As Macdonald argues, IT is analogous to R&D: as part of the woodwork, there can be no specific calculations of its output (Macdonald *et al.*, 2000).

At a different level, information technology can be viewed as a seed that breeds business value. The introduction of information technology focuses the attention of your employees, managers, business partners and even clients on specific aspects of your business. Does Deming's maxim of fifty years ago still ring true, 'Only that which gets measured gets managed. Only that which is managed is improved'? Regardless of the absolute objectivity of the measurement criteria, which is often open to a considerable degree of debate, the very fact that processes are under scrutiny often leads to increases in productivity. In focusing the attention of your business community on key aspects of your business, employees and partners alike more often than not adjust their priorities to demonstrate their contribution to the processes in question.

Box 3.5: When the chips are down . . .

Founded in 1968, the Intel Corporation's history has been coterminous with that of the Information Age. With thirty billion dollars in revenues, some eighty thousand employees, and 80% market penetration in the PC industry it is difficult to bet against a winning hand. Intel's major challenge is not the competition, but its own success, which has led to a saturated PC market. According to the company's new CEO, Paul Otellini, Intel's fate will no longer be assured by efficiently churning out faster and faster microprocessors. 'The history of the industry was the better-mousetrap syndrome: you build a faster thing and the world will beat a path to your doorstep,' he explains. 'But as the industry matured, that no longer became the best way to look at the problem'. When he suggested that his top management focus not on speed but on value, his chief financial officer reportedly laughed at him, 'Paul, no one is going to pay more for this stuff. It's just going to cost more to build it' (Rivlin and Markoff, 2004). Paul Otellini retorted that when the chips are down, management needs 'to understand what customers value. If we can bring something of more value, they'll pay for it.'

Moreover, the application of information technology to business challenges often leads to potential innovations in the practice of management. As demonstrated in the previous chapter, innovations in personal productivity, in the value chain, in reengineering and in the networked economy have been accompanied by, if not spurred by, corresponding evolutions in information technology. The practice of business process improvement itself has largely fed off progress in designing and deploying business information systems. Management consultants argue that organizational change is necessary to accompany IT implementations, and are more willing than not to provide the services for which they themselves have called. For the vast majority of enterprises today, the elaboration and practice of information technology have become virtually, if not physically, intertwined with management.

Finally, information technology has contributed to what and how we learn about business. The growing variety of client needs, the increasing complexity of our markets, and the globalization of the economy have rendered information technology indispensable in capturing, measuring, organizing and communicating what we need to know to survive, to compete and to thrive in business. As Lundvall and Johnson pointed out, technological innovation has created a learning economy based upon specialization and innovation as the fundamental building blocks of competitive advantage. 'It is through the combination of widespread ICT technologies, flexible specialization and innovation as a crucial means of competition ... that the learning economy gets firmly established. Firms start to learn how to learn' (Lundvall and Johnson, 1994). Information technology has slowly but surely changed the learning agenda: measuring the mechanics of producing products and services is no longer enough; business communities must learn how to measure their capacity for innovation in their responses to client demands.

What Have We Learned?

In this chapter we have explored how information technology has been deployed to measure business value. We have argued that 'productivity' cannot be reduced to quicker + cheaper = better because business value depends not only on how we measure performance but on the information technology we use to do so. Measures of business value have been designed to promote one of several objectives: to contextualize the meaning of value in a business community, to establish guidelines to compare business value, performance and productivity, or to design learning agendas for improving the value proportions of future products and services.

We have argued that measuring productivity isn't an end in itself but a means to search for business value. The impact of information technology depends more on how it is applied than in what we are trying to improve. In fact the best intentions concerning information technology may lead to poor business practice that actually pollutes the organization's value propositions. We would like to conclude by suggesting that information technology's most significant contribution is in its capacity to push us to continuously reassess the relationship between what we measure and how we wish to improve our business practice.

References

Brynjolfsson, Erik (1993) The productivity paradox of information technology, *Harvard Business Review*, Vol. 69, Iss. 1.

Carr, Nicolas (2003) *Does IT Matter?*, Boston, MA: Harvard Business School Press.

Davis, Gordon B. *et al.* (1993) Productivity for information technology investment in knowledge workers, in Rajiv D. Banker, Robert J. Kauffman and Mo A. Mahmood (Editors), *Strategic Information Technology Management Perspectives on Organizational Growth and Competitive Advantage*, Harrisburg, PA: Idea Publishing.

Diewert, W. E., and Kevin Fox (1999) Can measurement error explain the productivity paradox?, *Canadian Journal of Economics*, April.

Galford, Robert, and Anne Seibold Drapeau (2003) *The Enemies of Trust*, Boston, MA: Harvard Business School Press.

Handy, Charles (1995) Trust and the virtual organization, *Harvard Business Review*, May/June.

Hayzen, A. J., and J. M. Reeve (2000) Examining the relationships in productivity accounting, *Management Accounting Quarterly*, Summer, 32–39.

Lundvall, Bengt-Ake, and B. Johnson (1994) The Learning Economy, *Journal of Industry Studies*, Vol. 1, Iss. 2, 23–42.

Macdonald, Stuart, Pat Anderson and Dieter Kimbel (2000) Measurement or management?: Revisiting the productivity paradox of information technology, *Vierteljahrshefte zur Wirtschaftsforschung Jahrgang*, Vol. 4, 601–617.

McGehee, Tom (2001) *Whoosh*, Cambridge, MA: Perseus Publishing.

Parsons, John (2000) Current approaches to measurement within the service sector/white collar institutions, *Report on the APO Symposium on Productivity Measurement in the Service Sector, Kuala Lumpur, Malaysia, 1–4 August 2000*.

Quinn, James Brian, and Martin N. Baily (1994) Information technology: the key to service performance, *Brookings Review*, 22 June.

Rivlin, Gary, and John Markoff (2004) Can Mr. Chips transform Intel?, *The New York Times*, 12 September.

SEC (2002) Roundtable discussion on financial disclosure and auditor oversight, Securities and Exchange Commission, Tuesday March 6 (http://www.sec.gov/spotlight/roundtables/accountround030602.htm).

Smith, Fred (1999) Q&A: Fred Smith CEO of the FDX holding company that includes FedEx, *Internet Week*, October 25 (http://www.internetweek.com/trans/tr99-bs22.htm).

Solow, Robert S. (1987) We'd better watch out, *New York Times Book Review*, 12 July. (http://www.amrresearch.com/content/view.asp?pmillid=14452&docid=8857).

Strassman, Paul (1997) *The Squandered Computer*, New Canaan: Information Economics Press.

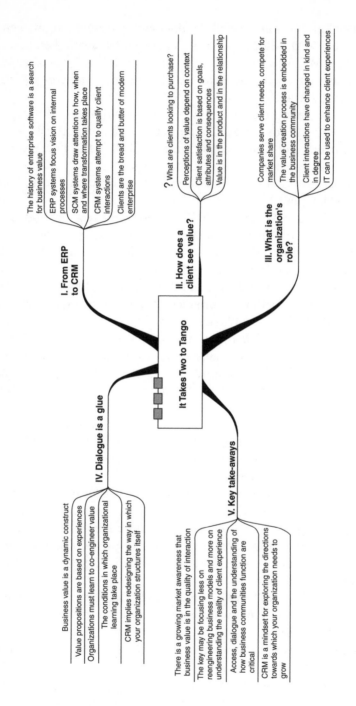

It Takes Two to Tango

I. From ERP to CRM

- The history of enterprise software is a search for business value
- ERP systems focus vision on internal processes
- SCM systems draw attention to how, when and where transformation takes place
- CRM systems attempt to qualify client interactions
- Clients are the bread and butter of modern enterprise

II. How does a client see value?

- ? What are clients looking to purchase?
- Perceptions of value depend on context
- Client satisfaction is based on goals, attributes and consequences
- Value is in the product and in the relationship

III. What is the organization's role?

- Companies serve client needs, compete for market share
- The value creation process is embedded in the business community
- Client interactions have changed in kind and in degree
- IT can be used to enhance client experiences

IV. Dialogue is a glue

- Business value is a dynamic construct
- Value propositions are based on experiences
- Organizations must learn to co-engineer value
- The conditions in which organizational learning take place
- CRM implies redesigning the way in which your organization structures itself

V. Key take-aways

- There is a growing market awareness that business value is in the quality of interaction
- The key may be focusing less on reengineering business models and more on understanding the reality of client experience
- Access, dialogue and the understanding of how business communities function are critical
- CRM is a mindset for exploring the directions towards which your organization needs to grow

4
It Takes Two (or More) to Tango

*D*errick, *a rising star of a major US-based supplier of home electronics equipment, knows how to close a sale. As the director of the corporation's Internet Sales Division in Europe, he asks his employees and colleagues to call him the 'animal'. He underlines that selling is the most important thing you need to know about his company. He suggests that selling is also the second most important thing you need to know, as well as the third. When questioned by his colleagues to explain how he is so successful at his job, he gives credit to the fact that his company assembles, distributes and services its own products. When I asked Derrick to push his reflection further, he gave me a tour of the production facility. He explained that he saw each product as a customer's heartbeat coming down the assembly line...*

Over the last decade, the focus of corporate investments in information technology has shifted from strengthening enterprise resource planning to developing client relationship management. This trend can be analysed as a growing recognition in the market that the foundation of business value is not in a company's product or service offer, but in the quality of interactions it maintains with its clients. In focusing on how organizations learn from their clients, we can gather a clearer picture of the importance of business value, the real impact of information technology and potential directions for organizational change and growth.

This move towards client relationship management, or CRM, has revealed the difficulties that information technology has in measuring value: the metrics of quicker and faster at the heart of the efficiency paradigm have been challenged by corporate needs to understand the nature of the relationships between the organization and its internal and external clients. This shift to CRM has also refocused management concerns from internal production processes to the external relationships that define business communities. Finally, this movement has brought to light the strengths and weaknesses of change management strategies: changes to the technological infrastructure are of little benefit if they do not enrich the nature of human interaction.

To examine how the trend towards client relationship management has impacted our perceptions of business value, we will begin this chapter with an overview of the evolution of 'process-centric' applications from enterprise resource planning to supply chain management to CRM. We will then investigate how the client perceives value, and the extent to which clients contribute to value creation. We will investigate how client-centric approaches have challenged how we use IT to capture business value, at what level we analyse processes, and where we measure the results. We will conclude this chapter with a discussion of the nature of the challenges that CRM introduces in developing change management strategies for your business.

We can suggest a number of questions for discussion and debate to better understand how we can improve our value propositions from a client's point of view:

- How does the client perceive business value?
- Do clients themselves create value?

- Why do efficiency metrics fail to capture client value?
- To what extent is IT capable of capturing these perceptions?
- What do organizations need to learn about how customers perceive value?

From Enterprise Resource Planning to Client Relationship Management

The recent history of enterprise software has been characterized by the search for business value. As discussed previously, IT infrastructures can be modelled to improve business strategy along any of three dimensions: increasing the visibility on the costs and benefits of organizational activities (enterprise resource planning); improving the organizational knowledge of client needs and objectives (customer relationship management); or optimizing the delivery of products or services (supply chain management). These three approaches are often referred to as process-centric applications since they imply that the business value of information technology can be found in improving one or several of these core processes. Corporate investments in these forms of enterprise software demonstrate the extent to which they have influenced managerial mindsets: they constitute today nearly three-quarters of corporate investments in software applications (Scott, 2002). Let us quickly look at how the three information strategies compare, and at the extent to which client relationship management reflects the strengths and weaknesses of the technologies as a whole.

Enterprise resource planning, or ERP, is a form of enterprise software intended to support and automate business processes. The market for enterprise resource planning software is estimated to be about $27 billion; almost all major corporations today run ERP software.[1] In

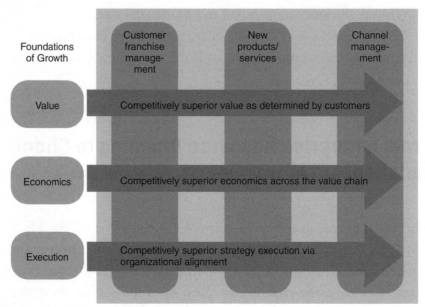

Figure 4.1 Opportunities for growth
Source: Accenture Consulting

Europe, the market is currently estimated to be around $1.9 billion, with estimates reaching $2.2 billion for 2007.[2] ERP usually regroups functions designed to improve manufacturing, distribution, project management, human resource management and finance. Descending from the MRP (material requirement planning) software of the 1980s, ERP systems have incorporated relational databases, client/server architectures and the Internet.

How have ERP systems influenced management practice? To begin with, enterprise resource planning focuses management attention on internal business processes rather than the interactions between the firm and its suppliers or clients. ERP systems are deployed to capture, aggregate and report quantitative data on manufacturing or service processes at specific points in time: the end of the day, the end of the week, or the end of the quarter. Investments in enterprise resource

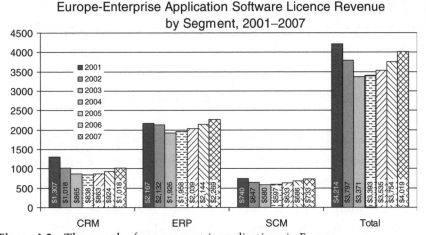

Figure 4.2 The growth of process-centric applications in Europe.
Source: Gartner Dataquest 'Enterprise Application Software by Industry: Europe, 2001–2007 (Pivot Table)' by Fabrizio Biscotti, Thomas Topolinski, Chad Eschinger, 13 January 2004. Reproduced by permission of Gartner, Inc.

planning are judged to be expensive: the total cost of ownership of an 'average' implementation is estimated to be 15 million euros.[3] The non-financial benefits are difficult to measure, and the payback period of five to seven years is considered quite long by many small and medium-sized firms.

These factors have tended to fuel the market for alternative approaches to enterprise software. One alternative approach is supply chain management, or SCM. SCM deals with the planning and execution issues involved in managing the functions of procurement of materials; transformation of these materials into intermediate and finished products; and distribution of these finished products to customers. The market for supply chain management software is estimated to be about $6 billion, including $596 million in Europe alone.[4] Such well-known corporations as Dell Computer, Amazon, Cisco and Wal-Mart have built their business models around supply chain approaches. SCM software has been developed to improve production and distribution planning, production scheduling and fore-casting. Descending from the total quality management approaches of W. E. Deming and Joseph Juran, SCM systems incorporate relational databases, client/server architectures and the Internet to focus on the issues of synchronization and optimization of distribution processes.

How have SCM systems influenced management practice? In contrast to enterprise resource planning, supply chain management has drawn management attention to how, whence and when raw materials are procured, manufactured and supplied to manufacturers and their distributors rather than focusing on internal processes. SCM systems are deployed to capture, aggregate and report quantitative data on distribution processes at specific periods of time: during the day, during the week, or during the production cycle. Investments in supply chain management are judged to be less costly than ERP: the processes between firms are usually less complex and easier to standardize than those inside the company itself. The concrete benefits have proved to be easier to measure; a payback period of one to three years is commonly accepted.

A more recent approach is client relationship management, or CRM. Originally coined by the Gartner Group, client relationship manage-ment refers to enterprise software applications that allow companies to manage the multiple aspects of customer relationships. Customer information acquired from sales, marketing, customer service and support is aggregated to help management understand how to nur-ture customer satisfaction and loyalty. The European market for client relationship management software today is $838 million and should reach $1018 billion by 2007. Descending from the simple client contact forms, CRM systems have adopted the same technological infrastructure of other process-centric systems to bring the client into the centre of corporate strategy.

How have CRM systems influenced management practice? In contrast to ERP and SCM, client relationship management draws management attention to the nature of a firm's client base and how they interact with the company rather than focusing on the mechanical processes of production and distribution. CRM systems are deployed to capture, analyse and communicate qualitative rather than quantitative data on client behaviour, objectives and needs. Investments in CRM are judged to be more profitable short-term investments than investments in other enterprise systems; improving service processes between a company and its clients is seen to be relatively straightforward and directly tied to the bottom line.

Enterprise resource planning, supply chain management and client relationship management are three distinct perspectives on how to build business value – through improving the firm's ability to understand the source of costs and benefits, to deliver the right product or service to the right person at the right time or to better understand clients' needs and objectives. In contrast to the other two approaches, CRM focuses on the qualitative aspects of business value and highlights the limits of the efficiency paradigm. CRM represents a distinctly new working framework for management, shifting the transactional focus of traditional business process reengineering in improving products to one favouring the quality of the interactions between the firm and its clients (see, for example, Sheth and Parvatiyar, 1995). In a management mindset in which production and distribution are frequently outsourced, client relationship management focuses on the bread and butter of modern enterprise: the customers themselves.

	ERP	SCM	CRM
Origins	MRP	Total Quality Management	Client contact systems
Measure	Quantitative static	Quantitative dynamic	Qualitative
Scope	Inside a firm	Between firms	Between firms and clients
Estimated ROI	5 to 7 years	1 to 3 years	6 months to 1 year

Figure 4.3 Three perspectives on how to build business value

How Does a Client See Value?

In the search for business value, CRM turns your attention away from the firm itself and towards your clients and customers. What do you see when looking at your clients and, more important, what do they see when looking at your company? What exactly are they looking to 'purchase', and how do they judge your value proposition? In their eyes, is value in the product or in the service; is it in the relationship they have with your company, or is it simply an impression in their heads? Will they be judging you product by product (or service by service), or do they weigh their cumulative experience with your company or its representatives?

Box 4.1: What is behind Sting?

As had often been the case over the last ten years, the pop music artist, Sting, had again filled up the Summum, the local concert hall in Grenoble, France. As always the audience was quite diverse: fans from the singer's days with Police mixed in with jazz enthusiasts and a large sprinkling of teenagers wanting to share a page of history. The popularity and longevity of Sting's music are testaments both to his talent and to his ability to relate to his audience through several generations. Which specific client needs does his music address? Was the audience present because the concert corresponded to their goals (budding stars wanting to learn the tricks of the trade), to the consequences of their presence (being able to listen to the live music), or to a feeling of community in sharing this evening with all those present?

How do this performer and his producer enrich the client experience? Are their customers looking for a product, a service or a place in a particular community? How can they motivate the accompanying musicians and crew to add value to the show? How will the customers judge the value of the performance (by the number of all-time hits sung, by the quality of the acoustics, by the richness of the conversation with the audience)? What can be learned by the singer from this experience that can be carried over to other concerts and/or products (interviews, lyrics, melodies)? What lessons can be drawn here for organizations in other markets?

Common sense dictates that customers purchase products to fulfil specific needs. Nonetheless the choice of most of the goods and the services we purchase, whether it be one particular type of car, stereo or computer, or today's lunch, do not correspond to any identifiable need. This point of view coincides with Bordieu's view that modern-day consumption is most often tied to the creation and maintenance of social status (Bordieu, 1984). Tzokas and Saren (1999) have concluded that the primary motivation for most of our purchases is not need but social rituals and conditioning. The fascination of a large majority of today's youth with branded merchandise certainly seems to back up these claims. It appears difficult to consider value a characteristic of a product when customers judge value on 'how good they look' rather than on the functionality of the product itself.

Customer perceptions of value are based on a number of factors that depend upon the nature of the purchase, upon the context and upon the relationship they maintain with the sales organization. Wilson and Jantrania (1994) suggest that clients judge value along three distinct dimensions: economic (what are the costs and benefits), strategic (does the product or service fill my needs) and/or behavioural (how does the purchase make me feel). Mattson (1990), for his part, suggests three generic dimensions of value: emotional (the feel-good factor), practical (does the purchase solve a problem) and logical (does the purchase correspond to my objectives) to describe how customers perceive value of services at different stages in the delivery process.

Contrastingly, Woodruf (1997) analyses client perceptions of value using a three-stage model of customer value involving goal-based, consequence-based and attribute-based satisfaction. He suggests that value from a client's point of view is a combination of both desired and perceived value that is based upon perceptions, preferences and evaluation. Take the example of a youth's enthusiasm for a certain brand of basketball shoes. On being questioned why his parents should pay twice the price of a non-branded shoe, the youth may well respond that he is convinced this brand of basketball shoes will help him one day become a professional basketball player (goal-based satisfaction). Alternatively, he may argue vehemently that the branded shoes will help him jump higher, run faster, manoeuvre more precisely than their non-branded equivalents (consequence-based satisfaction). Finally, the youth may admit freely that he "wouldn't be caught dead" in non-branded shoes, for what would his friends think (attribute-based satisfaction). As many parents would clearly attest, value seems to depend as much upon the customer's beliefs as it does upon the product or its manufacturer.

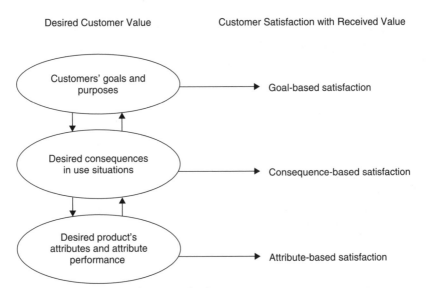

Figure 4.4   Customer perceptions of value
Source: R.B. Woodruf (1997) Customer value: the next source for competitive advantage, *Journal of the Academy of Marketing Science*, Vol. 25, Iss. 2, 139–153.

What part of value can be attributed to the purchase of a particular product and what part is attributable to the relationship that the customer or client maintains with the organization? Grönroos describes three categories of consumers, those that are solely interested in purchasing a product or service, those that passively engage in a relationship with a firm, and those actively engage in a relationship with the organization. Accordingly, he has proposed an analytical model for measuring how clients evaluate specific value propositions, as well as the value of client relationships. He suggests that the perceived value of an episode for a customer depends upon the benefits of the transaction itself with a weighting based upon the customer's perceptions of previous or expected benefits from the relationship (Grönroos, 1997). This type of analysis can go a long way to explaining why customers are willing to pay considerably more for business-class or first-class air tickets. The 'purchase' includes the customer's evaluation of the wait in the check-in queue, the eventual use of the executive lounge, and the expectations of better in-flight service. From a customer's point of view, value depends both on the price of the solution and on the perception of relationship costs (or benefits).

Table 4.1 Customer perceptions of value

$$\text{Total episode value} = \frac{\text{Episode benefits} + \text{Relationship benefits}}{\text{Episode sacrifice} + \text{Relationship sacrifice}}$$

$$\text{Customer perceived value (CPV)} = \frac{\text{Core solution} + \text{Additional services}}{\text{Price} + \text{Relationships costs}}$$

$$\text{Customer perceived value (CPV)} = \text{Core value} + \text{or} - \text{Added value}$$

Source: Grönroos (1997). Reproduced by permission of Westburn Publishers Ltd.

What Is Your Organization's Role in Value Creation?

If the client's role in the creation of business value seems clear, what role does the company play? Marketing theorists have long argued that the organization plays essentially two roles in generating value. On the one hand, the company focuses on serving customer needs profitably, and thus organizes its resources to optimize the delivery of products and services. On the other hand, each company competes for clients within its market, and thereby aims to create and maintain a competitive advantage over other companies. In both cases, as Day and Wensley (1983) point out, customers are viewed as the 'ultimate prize gained at the expense of rivals in many ways other than by simply offering a better match of products to customer needs'. As Tzokas and Saren (1999) conclude, traditional approaches to marketing view the customer as a trophy that is detached from the value creation process.

How can we reconcile this view of the customer as an object with our conceptions of the client as the central actor in determining business value? A number of proponents of relationship marketing argue today that the value creation process is not part of a company but of a business community. Products and services alone do not produce value; business value is dependent upon client experience, expectations and needs. Companies at best co-produce value in relationships with consumers, customers and clients. As Wilkstrom (1996) argues, the organization's objectives should be designing systems of activities within which customers can create their own value.

Box 4.2: Carbon copies

Digital technologies have infiltrated almost every activity of modern enterprise. Multiple fax machines, scanners, copiers and printers can be found in even the smallest companies. As the cost of the hardware has diminished to the point where their purchase can be justified for almost any office, the cost of the ink cartridges have provided a pot of gold to the suppliers of these technologies. The *Financial Times* has estimated that if the hardware is often offered at considerably less than $200 a unit, the ink is billed around $2000 a litre! It is of little wonder that a supplier like HP produces gross margins of close to 80% in this sector.[5]

What is considered a gold mine by some may be considered strip mining by others. There seems to be an inherent link between the growing ability to capture, produce and communicate information and the increasing kilos of drafts, copies and faxes that have inundated the workplace. Unfortunately it has proved to be difficult to demonstrate the link between the rising costs of maintaining and operating these digital devices and corresponding increases in productivity, innovation or creativity. In a recent bid to the major international carrier, DT Services faced a seemingly unsolvable riddle: how can a supplier demonstrate value in providing the maintenance of 1400 digital devices which already produce 60 million copies and 110 million printouts a year? DT Services proposed an innovative and winning bid by offering the group the hardware at no cost, and billing a per unit transaction fee (scans and/or copies). As a result, each business unit may use the digital devices freely, but is strongly encouraged to justify the corresponding business benefits.

How have clients changed? Prahalad and Ramaswamy (2004) argue that, in an interconnected, networked economy, client interactions have changed both in kind and in degree. To begin with, clients have unprecedented access to information and knowledge about prices, products, technologies and business, and as a result can take more informed decisions. Further, this information is not bound to any one culture or market; globalization has opened consumers' eyes to ideas, practices and reactions from around the world. The development of the Internet in particular and telecommunications in general has created a modern-day Pandora's Box: unparalleled curiosity and openness among customers, clients and consumers. In such a climate, the authors argue, not only can clients better discriminate in choosing products and services, but client networks are in themselves a source of empowerment. Consumers increasingly directly participate in how value is defined, created and measured. Blogs, clips, discussion forums and websites reflect and share public opinion and debate. As a result, companies can no longer claim to create value through their unique efforts in marketing and sales. Internal and external clients, whether they are consumers, business partners or competitors, interact with management in 'co-creating' value.

To what extent can information technology be used to enhance client experiences? As argued in Chapter 2, 'The House of Mirrors', information technology can be used in several ways to support business value. In regard to client relationship management, IT can be used to capture data and information on customer needs and expectations. IT can help to measure how clients perceive the added value of your products, services and organization. Information technology can be used to aggregate client data, to search for patterns of client behaviour and preferences. Information systems can be an integral part of value propositions designed to heighten the client experience. Finally, information technology can be used to reinforce the process of communicating value to and from your clients.

Dialogue Is the Glue that Holds Business Communities Together

In this light, business value can be modelled as a dynamic construct which eludes easy measurement. Operational measures, such as efficiency, utilization and quality, capture only part of the picture of how organizations interact with clients. The characteristics of any one product, service or team are not adequate to explain how client relationships are initiated, nurtured and prosper. Business value, from a client perspective, can be analysed on any one of several levels. Clients interact with your organization through their enquiries, their purchases and their dealings with your company and its representatives. Your clients compete with each other, fuelling and justifying the need for your organization's products and services. Finally, clients also interact with each other – their opinions and observations concerning their suppliers and the market can help to form and modify individual perceptions of value.

As the focus of value propositions shifts from products and services to experiences, business communities become forums for conversation and interactions between customers, consumers, clients and your organization. It is this access, dialogue and understanding of business that is central to value creation. The importance of dialogue as a foundation for value creation should not be underestimated. Hazen (1984) suggests that dialogue is critical both to contributing to individual empowerment and to changing management process. Schein (1993) argues that dialogue is 'a way of building a basis for mutual understanding and trust by uncovering the basic cognitive processes that underlie individual and group assumptions'. As such, dialogue between suppliers, distributors and clients influences not only what functions and features they may or may not consider valuable, but also the underlying belief structures that determine how and why we react to specific business challenges.

Box 4.3: Keeping in time with the music

Thomas Siebel founded Siebel in 1993 to help companies manage their customer relationships and help management better understand consumer buying habits. A long list of major corporations, including General Motors, Sprint and Procter & Gamble have purchased Siebel's products, making client relationship management a multimillion-dollar market. Nonetheless, the company has suffered in the last few years: its stock is down 93% since September 2000, and its revenue is barely half what it was in 2001. Even more alarmingly, whereas its competitors have grown their market shares, the company is still struggling to understand its clients' current needs and objectives.

J. Michael Lawrie, the company's new CEO, is convinced that Siebel can succeed if the company finds ways to innovate in staying a step or two ahead of the competition. As the industry analyst Paul Greenberg notes, Siebel may be its own worst enemy: 'The fundamental issue for Siebel has always been the culture more than its products. There was this shark sales culture where you were encouraged to do anything to get the deal and in a sense the hell with the customer.'[6] Paradoxically, Siebel's fortunes depend less on its ability to produce innovative products than on its ability to improve the dialogue between its sales force and its customers. As many might conclude, it takes (at least) two to tango.

Perhaps even more importantly, dialogue is fundamental to how organizations learn to co-engineer value with their customers. Exactly how do individuals and organizations learn to co-engineer value? In their groundbreaking work in the late 1970s, Argyris and Schön (1978) distinguished individual from organizational learning and also distinguished several levels of learning within the organization. The authors suggested that learning involves the detection and correction of error. Whenever an error or a difference is noted between current and desired states in our working environment, we as individuals, groups and/or organizations will try to correct the situation. If our actions are undertaken without questioning or altering the underlying rules or norms of the firm or of the market, the learning is single-loop. If, on the other hand, our actions involve examining and altering the principles and values that normally guide our actions, the learning can be considered double-loop. Dodgson (1993) suggests that organizations use both types of learning in building, supplementing and organizing 'knowledge and routines around their activities and within their cultures and adapt and develop organizational efficiency by improving the use of the broad skills of their workforces'.

In what conditions will organizational learning take place? More often than not organizational structures and norms limit our opportunities to learn from our clients. Corporate vision encourages us to focus on the 'big picture' rather than to dwell upon signals from our clients that the company might be out of focus. Quality standards offer us norms of acceptable behaviour rather than encouragements to think 'out of the box' to solve client challenges. Management's classic precepts of command and control encourage conformity and obedience rather than creativity and innovation. It is little wonder that, when faced with declining profits and/or a declining client base, many managers will persist in old habits, and/or argue that the solution must be in going quicker and cheaper. Nevis *et al.* (1995) argue to the contrary that the key factor in learning is individual and/or organizational awareness that there is a problem.

In what conditions do organizations engage in what Argyris calls deutero-learning, or learning to learn? Deutero-learning may be tied to a recognition of the fact that adhering too closely to strategy carved in stone, or vaunting too loudly examples of corporate 'wins', can actually block learning. In a rapidly changing economic environment with increasingly diverse client needs there may not be one best practice or any solution that will forever stand the test of time. Nevis and his co-authors, in studying Motorola, Mutual Investment Corporation, Electricité de France and Fiat, go on to identify seven different learning styles and ten different facilitating factors that influence learning. Awareness of client challenges and objectives can help your organization realize that learning needs to occur and that the appropriate environment and processes need to be created (Argyris, 1994). Client relationship management is not about structuring the relationship between your organization and its clients; it implies redesigning the way in which your organization is structured itself.

In using Prahalad and Ramaswamy's (2004) analysis as a focal point, a manager's guide to more effective client relationships might begin with the following questions. How do your clients participate in the process of value creation? What are the components of value creation: your products, your services, or the client experience? How does the quality of their interaction with your sales force, distributors and technical staff affect their appreciation of the client experience? How does the business community's ability to deal with new challenges (penury, saturation, new sources of competition, customers etc.) affect each client's appreciation of value? Can your organization create an environment that permits your collaborators (including your clients) to sufficiently create and innovate to strengthen the relationships within your business community?

What Have We Learned?

A number of points for discussion can be drawn from this chapter. To begin with, the trend towards client relationship management underlines a growing market awareness that the foundation of business value is not in a company's product or service offer, but in the quality of interactions it maintains with its clients. In contrast to other process-centric technologies, client relationship management draws management attention to the nature of a firm's client base and how the clients interact with the company, rather than focusing on the mechanical processes of production and distribution. In focusing on the qualitative aspects of business value, CRM represents a distinctly new working framework for management: it shifts the transactional focus of traditional business process reengineering in improving products to one favouring the quality of the interactions between the firm and its clients. In a management mindset bred on the efficiency paradigm of quicker and cheaper, client relationship management focuses on the bread and butter of modern enterprise: the customers themselves.

Customer perceptions of value are based on a number of factors that depend upon the nature of the purchase, upon the context, and upon the relationship they maintain with the sales organization. From this perspective, what role can the company play in the creation of value? Companies co-produce value through relationships by designing systems of activities within which consumers, customers and clients can create their own value. Access, dialogue and the understanding of how business communities function are central to value creation. Fundamental to managing organizations today is the understanding of how your company and its collaborators learn to learn. Client relationship management is not a form of information technology for capturing client information; it is a mindset for exploring the directions in which your organization needs to grow in its business community.

Notes

1. International Data Corporation, Worldwide ERP Application Market 2004–2008 Forecast: First look at top 10 vendors (IDC #31269).
2. Source: Gartner/Dataquest. Figures have been supplied by Oracle EMEA.
3. According to the Meta Group, quoted in Mello (2002).
4. AMR Research's European Applications Market Analytix Report, 2001–2006.
5. As reported in *La Tribune*, 'HP en ordre de marche pour conquérir des marchés', September 8, 2004, p. 36.
6. As reported in Rivlin (2004).

References

Argyris, Chris (1994) Good communication that blocks learning, *Harvard Business Review*, July–August, 77–85.
Argyris, Chris, and Donald A. Schön (1978) *Organizational Learning: A Theory of Action Perspective*, Reading, MA: Addison-Wesley.
Bordieu, Pierre (1984) *La Distinction: Critique Sociale du Jugement*, Paris: Minuit.
Day, G. S., and R. Wensley (1983) Marketing theory with a strategic orientation. *Journal of Marketing*, Vol. 47, Iss. 4, 79–89.

Dodgson, M. (1993) Organizational learning: a review of some literatures, *Organization Studies*, Vol. 14, Iss. 3, 375–394.

Grönroos, Christian (1997) Value-driven relational marketing: from products to resources and competencies, *Journal of Marketing Management*, Vol. 13, Iss. 5, 407–419.

Hazen, M. A. (1984) A radical humanist perspective of interorganizational relationships. *Human Relations*, Vol. 47, Iss. 4, 393–415.

Mattson, J. (1990) Measuring inherent product values, *European Journal of Marketing*, Vol. 24, Iss. 9, 25–38.

Mello, Adrian (2002) ERP fundamentals ERP's hidden costs, Inside ERP: Special Report, *ZD Net*, 7 February (http://techupdate.zdnet.com/techupdate/stories/main/0,14179,2844319-3,00.html).

Nevis, Edwin C., Anthony J. DiBella and Janet M. Gould (1995) Understanding organizations as learning systems, *Sloan Management Review*, Vol. 36, Iss. 2, 73–85.

Prahalad, C. K., and Venkat Ramaswamy (2004) The future of competition: co-creating unique value with customers, *Harvard Business School Press*, 18 February.

Rivlin, Gary (2004) The customer relationship expert takes a dose of its own medicine, *New York Times*, 13 September.

Schein, E. H. (1993) On dialogue, culture and organizational learning, *Organizational Dynamics*, Vol. 22, Iss. 2, 40–52.

Scott, Fenella (2002) The decline in 2002 IT spending: is it perception or reality?, *AMR Research*, 3 July.

Sheth, J. N., and A. Parvatiyar (1995) Relationship marketing in consumer markets: antecedents and consequences, *Journal of the Academy of Marketing Science*, Vol. 23, Iss. 4, 255–271.

Tzokas, Nikolaos, and Michael Saren (1999) Value transformation in relationship marketing, *Australasian Marketing*, Vol. 7, Iss. 1, 52–62.

Wilkstrom, S. (1996) Value creation by company–consumer interaction, *Journal of Marketing Management*, Vol. 12, 359–374.

Wilson, D. T., and S. Jantrania (1994) Understanding the value of a relationship, *Asia–Australia Marketing Journal*, Vol. 1, 55–56.

Woodruf, R. B. (1997) Customer value: the next source for competitive advantage, *Journal of the Academy of Marketing Science*, Vol. 25, Iss. 2, 139–153.

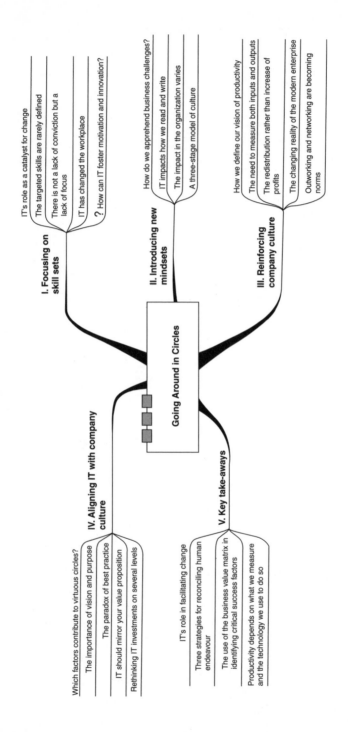

Going Around in Circles

I. Focusing on skill sets
- IT's role as a catalyst for change
- The targeted skills are rarely defined
- There is not a lack of conviction but a lack of focus
- IT has changed the workplace
- *?* How can IT foster motivation and innovation?

II. Introducing new mindsets
- How do we apprehend business challenges?
- IT impacts how we read and write
- The impact in the organization varies
- A three-stage model of culture

III. Reinforcing company culture
- How we define our vision of productivity
- The need to measure both inputs and outputs
- The redistribution rather than increase of profits
- The changing reality of the modern enterprise
- Outworking and networking are becoming norms

IV. Aligning IT with company culture
- Which factors contribute to virtuous circles?
- The importance of vision and purpose
- The paradox of best practice
- IT should mirror your value proposition
- Rethinking IT investments on several levels

V. Key take-aways
- IT's role in facilitating change
- Three strategies for reconciling human endeavour
- The use of the business value matrix in identifying critical success factors
- Productivity depends on what we measure and the technology we use to do so

5
Going Around in Circles

A *s has often been the case, a Scandinavian telecommuni-*
cations operator hoped to leverage IT in creating a new
corporate culture for their joint venture with an American
computer manufacturer. They nominated a young French engineer of
Swedish descent and gave her three missions: to oversee the technical
implementation of the enterprise system, to manage the training of
each department in best practices, and to communicate as widely
as possible on the business value of this information technology.
As intelligent as she was persuasive, the engineer and her managers
were confident in her ability to drive the project forward. Although the
technical implementation and training went largely as planned, she
met increasing difficulties in communicating the added value of this
investment to both management and external stakeholders. Much to
her dismay, the new IT system did not broaden the vision of either
employees or their management. To the contrary, many complained
of the rigidity and the extra work required by the new system, which
was reducing their workspace to a high-tech equivalent of Charlie
Chaplin's Modern Times . . .

Over the last several decades, the principal focus of management has
shifted from supervising human and physical resources to improving
how firms design, market and service their product offers. This shift

from outcomes to process requires a clear understanding of how people work together effectively, both within their firms and with their external clients. New resources, new organizational structures and new technology can be motors for change.

Managing organizational change is not about 'driving' change throughout the organization, but helping people accept new approaches to work and the workplace. The dynamics of change can lead either to a virtuous circle, reinforcing an organization's ability to respond to evolving market conditions, or to a vicious circle, disrupting organizational focus, eroding competitive position and leading inevitably to problems with the bottom line.

To explore information technology's role in supporting change management strategies in business, we will begin this chapter with an examination of IT's potential impact on individuals, firms and markets. We will then investigate the potential consequences of technology-driven change. We will conclude this chapter with a discussion of why IT appears to contribute to the desired outcomes in certain cases, and produce exactly the opposite effects in others.

We can suggest a number of questions for discussion and debate to better understand how investments in information technology affect corporate productivity:

- How has information technology influenced how we work and how we think about our workplace?
- To what extent does IT reflect or distort how we envision and embody company culture?
- In what conditions does information technology lead to vicious circles of apathy, underperformance and declining profitability?

- In what conditions does IT lead to virtuous circles of creativity, innovation and passion?
- How can you best leverage IT to support change management strategies in your organization?

Focusing on Skill Sets

Information technology is commonly viewed today as a catalyst for change. Private enterprise is estimated to have spent more than $1.2 trillion on information technology in the United States alone from 1995 to 2000 (Manyika and Nevens, 2002). Information and communications industries are growing more than five percentage points faster than the economy as a whole and drive total economic growth in industrial economies by more than 15%. Economists suggest that information technology is responsible today for the creation of one in every four new jobs in Europe, and in the coming decade half of all jobs will be in industries that are either major producers or intensive users of information technology products and services. As a result, public and private actors alike plead in favour of a 'digitally literate' population, capable of producing an 'entrepreneurial, service-oriented culture' consistent with the Information Society (European Commission, 2000).

To what extent can technologically driven change be a catalyst for improving organizational performance? At the heart of this proposition is an assumption concerning the extent to which organizations can and need to change to achieve the targeted business outcomes. Drawing parallels from popular literature, management gurus regularly suggest three methods for reconciling human endeavour, modern organizations and the market. One school of thought puts forward strategies for influencing how we work by describing relevant 'skill sets' and relevant training strategies. A second school argues that managers must introduce new 'mindsets' concerning the workplace before employees will accept that they have to change their skill sets. A third school argues that mindsets depend upon deeper-rooted collective beliefs about company culture, and that change management strategies need to begin by addressing the vision of what the company represents and how it wishes to develop.

Box 5.1: Is information technology the safest way to business value?

Sarbjit watched with growing satisfaction as shoppers queued at the newly converted Morrison supermarket. Ever since the £3 billion acquisition of the Safeway chain, financial analysts had questioned the wisdom of CEO Ken Morrison's plans. As a result, one of Great Britain's leading retail chains had seen its stock depreciate by nearly £2 billion in the previous six months alone. Industry analysts have concluded that the store-conversation programme will ultimately determine the success or failure of this joint venture.

In financial ventures of this kind, information technology plays a critical role in leveraging acquisitions: IT can rationalize and standardize business processes while focusing employees, managers and partners on a new company vision. In this particular case, Sir Ken decided to do just the opposite: he abandoned Safeway's state-of-the-art supply chain management application in favour of Morrison's traditional paper-based system. Sarbjit, the former manager of a Safeway store in London, feels that creating a collaborative-based culture will be the key to success. The paper-based system helps him focus on his clients rather than on technology: 'I can run my shop now' (Fletcher, 2004).

Information technology has had an undeniable impact on how we work, both collectively and individually. The 'success' stories of automated processes in the automobile, computer and retail industries are widely publicized. Managers use information technology to optimize the major processes of modern business: sales, marketing, logistics, finance and human resource management. The 'e-business' bubble has indeed burst, and as a result information technology has left its watermark on the way we work. Critics of the 'Net' economy were only partially right in arguing that e-business would be a passing fashion; the 'e' has disappeared as information technology now flows through the heart of business itself.

In such a context, managers and employees alike rightfully question which skills need to be acquired to use information technology effectively. 'Digital literacy' is now considered as basic a skill as reading and writing. The European Council recommended a European deadline of December 2003 for all pupils being 'digitally literate' by the time they leave school. These efforts have translated 'digital literacy' into a set of basic 'competencies': (a) mastering the Internet and multimedia resources; (b) using these new resources to learn and acquire new skills; and (c) acquiring key skills; such as collaborative working, creativity, multidisciplinary adaptability, intercultural communication and problem-solving.

If everyone is in general agreement about the big picture, the devil is in the detail. 'Technical literacy is quickly becoming as important as the ability to read. Yet our educational systems do not treat it as such. Too often, IT training is seen as ancillary, not central, to the educational process. The pace of technological change is far outstripping the investment we are making in our future'. The fundamental difficulty does not appear to be a lack of conviction as much as a lack of focus. If the skill set for technical jobs has been fairly well defined, the soft 'IT' skills needed by both the manager and employee (and perhaps the client) are open to wide debate. If innovations in information technology suggest that we must learn to write, read, work and learn differently, the challenge is in understanding exactly what we need to learn.

A second consideration that needs to be taken into account is that IT has changed the very nature of the workplace. Many companies invariably focus their IT investments to reduce the interaction costs that consume 40 to 60% of their staff's time. Certain 'jobs' are directly threatened (secretarial services, factory line work, bank tellers), and others have been greatly transformed (accounting, stock management, programming, and of course consulting and management). Coordinators, expediters, order-entry clerks, schedulers, customer service representatives are other examples of employment designed mainly to fill the gaps in information between the organization's departments and the firm, its suppliers and customers (Manyika and Nevens, 2002).

If particular skills can be specified, taught and eventually assimilated, the corresponding competencies needed to help the enterprise prosper form a far more subtle equation. Teaching and learning effective IT competencies require an understanding not only of trade skills, but of personal motivation, experience, values and vision in our daily work. As we will discuss in Chapter 7, 'Soldiers of the Shadows', this reality would seem to require us to abandon the distinction between 'hard' technical and 'soft' organizational skills. It makes no more sense to teach information technology today without discussing the business context in which it is applied than to discuss business skills without reference to information technology.

We can also question to what extent fostering motivation and innovation constitute basic business skills. If they do, to what extent does information technology support these skills? Two observations seem to suggest that current IT practice does indeed need to be put to question. Because of the hands-on-the-keyboard approach to training, the behavioural consequences of introducing new IT are rarely addressed in IT training courses. As a consequence, information technology is often perceived by 'end-users' as a substitute for human skill, and in such a context is considered more as a threat than as a source for personal motivation. Even more importantly, the very nature of current IT systems encourages learning by repetition; information systems structure potential solutions based on past experience. If innovation means finding new solutions to old problems, or even framing problems in a different light, most IT systems today are designed explicitly or implicitly to inhibit innovation.

Introducing New Mindsets

A second strategy for improving organizational performance revolves around influencing how we apprehend and resolve business challenges. As information technology permeates modern business, two complementary tendencies have developed. On the one hand, IT suppliers attempt to seamlessly integrate diverse platforms, software and business logic. As a result, information technology 'solutions' have become increasingly complex. On the other hand, user interfaces have become increasingly intuitive, permitting a larger and larger population of managers to use information technology efficiently. This apparent contradiction is welcomed by a large percentage of the business community who would heartily agree with the truism, 'Computers should be like automobiles. We need to know how to drive a car, not how it works.' Are there dangers in taking this analogy at face value?

One of the most visible effects of information technology is its impact on how business people read and write. Information systems in general, and the web in particular, have put a treasure house of information at our fingertips. Software, from simple spreadsheets to complex accounting systems, allow us to tackle mathematical calculations that manually are largely out of the question. The advent of larger, faster and cheaper computer systems has influenced how we receive, read and analyze this wealth of information. Calculators have become crutches for producing results quickly without having to analyze the underlying problems. Though few doubt that information technology produces results, good management often proves to be less about using IT well than about understanding the roots of business problems.

Electronic mail provides another case in point. The invention of e-mail has been seen as a godsend for many businesses in that it greatly increased the speed and breadth of corporate communications while decreasing transmission costs. Many managers receive dozens of messages a day and correspond with hundreds of contacts at all levels of their business and social communities. The advantages of this technological innovation need to be weighed against the disadvantages that it has brought. Few objectives, rules or norms have been established in most businesses to help managers effectively use electronic mail. Employees and management alike can spend hours a day reading and responding to mail that may or may not help them reach business objectives. With the introduction of the Internet, managing e-mail at home, in meetings and in conferences interferes with the social interactions that these environments were originally intended to foster. The tone, the depth and the quality of messages seem to suffer proportionately.

Presentation graphics provide an even more telling example. Presentation packages such as PowerPoint™ have significantly enriched management's possibilities of providing animated, colourful and structured presentations. The success of such software has reached a point where it is now rare to participate in a meeting or conference in which the speaker does not use an electronic presentation. Unfortunately, many speakers are privileging their sophisticated graphics to the detriment of fostering communication. Presentation graphics packages are designed to display a message, and not, unfortunately, to capture feedback from the audience. Moreover, top management and clients alike are increasingly questioning whether complex business problems and solutions can be reduced to 'three points a slide'. Faced with conference participants who frequently express a preference for receiving electronic copies of the presentation after the conference rather than taking notes, speakers often wonder why they needed to present their ideas at all.

Box 5.2: Too much of a good thing?

David, the managing director of a leading British subcontractor for the aeronautic industry was increasingly upset with the presentation skills his managers displayed in the company's monthly review meetings. He noticed that his managers were much better at lecturing than listening, that all problems seemed to be reduced to three points per slide, and that the choice of colours for slides seemed to get more attention than the nuances of the company's business challenges. David expressed his frustration to the training manager who promptly allocated a budget for in-house training on the market-leading software, PowerPoint™. As the months passed, the managing director's frustration grew. He authorized a second training budget directly for each manager, most of whom in turn enrolled in advanced external courses on PowerPoint. The managing director's frustration grew further still, and he finally took the decision to take things into his own hands. Presentation graphics software is now banned from company meetings. The managers are evaluated on how effectively they enter into a dialogue with their colleagues.

Process-centric applications (such as enterprise resource planning or supply chain management suites of software) offer a more subtle but even more powerful demonstration. Process-centric software packages are installed to align the actual management of key business processes with predefined best practices. These packages ideally provide the end-user with a unique interface to access information throughout the firm and, potentially, the business community. As laudable as this logic may be, in reality many end-users work around what they perceive to be needlessly complex systems to continue to do 'business as usual'. Those that do adopt the new logic may do so at the expense of the very company culture that breeds innovation and contributes to competitive advantage. Faced with time and training constraints, the workforce often focuses on capturing information rather than using the system to learn business logic. As well designed as these packages may be, certain management mindsets can render the adage 'garbage in, garbage out' self-fulfilling.

Why does information technology provide the foundations for enhancing business performance in certain cases, and produce exactly the opposite effects in others? Business value is built up through the continual enhancement of an organization's ability to deal with business challenges in a manner compatible with its identity or organizational culture. By culture we mean the processes by which individuals and organizations bind rituals, climate, values and behaviours together into a coherent whole. All organizations have an organizational culture; some, because of their history, their market or their resources, may have more than one. Coming to grips with how these processes function from one organization to the next is critical in understanding how information technology can support the creation of business value.

Schein's three-stage model of organizational culture can help to elucidate how this process works. The first level, *artefacts*, includes the visible features of the workplace, such as activities, rituals, jargon and office layouts. The second level, *values and beliefs*, includes organizational views about what is good and bad which are used to monitor, evaluate and regulate organizational and market behaviour. The third level, *basic assumptions*, represents individual fundamental visions of reality – what 'truths' individual employees and managers hold about people and the world (Schein, 1992). The introduction of information technology is often aimed at modifying the visible features of an organization without taking into account the underlying values, beliefs and assumptions that explain how work gets done. Information technology may leave the belief structure intact, minimizing the intended organizational impact, or, worse, may contradict the implicit values and assumptions held by individuals and have a negative impact.

Reinforcing Company Culture

A third strategy for improving performance focuses on how management and employees define their vision of productivity itself. As previously mentioned, productivity is traditionally viewed as the ratio of inputs to outputs. Managers have sought to use information technology as a value lever for improving productivity. The vision of how IT improves productivity has changed radically in recent years. Originally 'IT productivity' was envisioned as a corollary of labour productivity: investments in IT allowed companies to rationalize their workforce resulting in a higher output per employee. Visions of IT value have progressively replaced the claims for IT productivity based upon more rational uses of resources in the 1980s, with a better understanding of corporate strategy in the 1990s, and with improved management and information systems in the 2000s.

We have identified several difficulties that obscure a clear vision of information technology's impact on productivity. To begin with, managers and academics alike have had difficulties quantifying and qualifying the measurements of the inputs and outputs of both labour and capital. Should the impact of IT be measured only in terms of lower production costs, or improvements in the quality and responsiveness of the resulting product or service offer? On another level, the effects of information technology are not necessarily immediate: improvements may come over time as employees and managers adapt and adjust practices, procedures and processes to new tools and techniques. The introduction of enterprise resource planning systems most often results in productivity losses in the short term, but may well contribute to stronger foundations for productivity increases in the middle to long term.

Moreover, information technology may lead to a redistribution of profits among clients rather than a direct increase in profits for the firm. The introduction of automatic teller machines in the banking sector has led not necessarily to higher profits, but to increases in customer satisfaction. Moreover, the impact of information technology can be diminished by management's misunderstanding the nature of organizational complexity and the necessary conditions for change. As computer systems evolve from simple calculating machines to support systems for diverse business processes, new forms of management thinking need to be developed.

The reality of modern enterprise has indeed changed with the introduction of information technology. Delocalization has become a common managerial practice as information technology has facilitated movements of capital, labour and physical goods. The nature of the product offers have also evolved as competitive advantage is increasingly dependent on the nature of the service offer rather than on the intrinsic characteristics of the firm's products themselves. These transformations have led many firms to question their core competencies: competitive position depends less on what they do than on their ability to adapt quickly to new forms of productivity.

A new vision of IT productivity may well be constructed to come to grips with these new forms of productivity. Information technology is being applied to capture, to document and to redesign business processes, not around physical products but around services directly tied to client visions of value. The traditional relationships of command and control within the organization are gradually giving way to networks of influence and collaboration that extend from within the firm across business communities themselves. Outsourcing and networking are becoming norms rather than exceptions as modern enterprise is being reconfigured around new images of production and profitability.

Aligning Information Technology with Company Culture

In certain conditions IT serves as an effective lever of virtuous circles of passion, innovation and business value. In other conditions, similar types of information technology are accelerators of vicious circles of apathy, underperformance and the destruction of company culture. What factors contribute to successful implementations of technology? And what circumstances tend to undermine these value propositions? The Business Value Matrix™, introduced in Chapter1, can provide a certain number of elements.

Where does value come from? One fundamental premise introduced by the Business Value Matrix™ is that companies, as represented by their stakeholders, have intimate beliefs concerning the source of value in their organizations. While certain representatives believe that value is a characteristic of human endeavour, others see value as the result of process, and still others attribute value to technological 'innovation'. As we have argued in Chapter 2, 'The House of Mirrors', successive generations of information technology have provoked contrasting images of ourselves and our organizations. Introducing new forms of information technology into our companies can either reinforce positive images of our jobs, our visions and our future, or conversely can contradict the vision and purpose we attach to our workplace.

Box 5.3: Travelling in class

In the eyes of most CFOs, business class travel is not as attractive as it once was. Faced with increasing pressures to keep costs

---

down, it has become increasingly difficult for managers to justify paying premium tickets on flights just for a better meal and a little extra leg-room. Many companies have tried to restrict business travel altogether, encouraging management to explore the advantages of both web and telephone conferences. Beyond the classic arguments of time and money, long-haul flights leave managers out of touch, out of work and unproductive for large parts of each day.

To meet this challenge, Lufthansa has recently introduced an on-board computer network that offers wireless, broadband connection to business travellers. Baptized FlyNet®, the network communicates via 10 geostationary satellites in orbit 36 000 kilometres from the earth. A number of wide area network access points on the plane ensure controlled transmission and reception to and from the passengers' mobile devices. The company estimates that business travellers on international flights will be willing to spend up to an average of four hours communicating with their teams, business partners and clients. Assuming that their time is worth a minimum of 250 euros an hour, such productivity gains can provide a powerful financial argument for travelling in class.

Consider technology that is designed to standardize processes within the organization around notions of best practice. Process-centric information systems based on principles of enterprise resource planning or supply chain management, as well as many accounting and sales packages, are implemented to encourage the development of norms of acceptable employee behaviour. They are based on beliefs that organizations should be designed around management rules rather than client relationships. They discourage and even penalize individual initiatives to meet the specific needs of internal or external clients. They inhibit creativity and innovation that contest established practice and commonly accepted ideas concerning productivity and value. For organizational stakeholders who believe human endeavour to be more important than process, these technologies may very well lead to vicious circles of declining motivation and profit.

Does information technology mirror how your organization provides value to its customers? In many organizations the technological infrastructure mirrors organizational charts: choices of hardware, software and training are dedicated to the specific needs of each function in the firm: sales, marketing, engineering, manufacturing and administration. In some organizations the technological infrastructure mirrors the design of core processes: choices of hardware, software and training are made to facilitate the flow of information from initial client demands through to the conception, production and delivery of products or services designed to meet client objectives. In still other organizations technology seems to have a life of its own; technology is purchased mostly to repair or improve weaknesses in the current installation, adding features and functionalities that were 'missing' from the existing infrastructure. In each of these cases, you can justifiably question whether technology mirrors the culture and the vision of the organization, whether it reflects how work actually gets done, and whether it helps you deal with the reality of your business challenges.

If formal organizational structures accurately depict the workings of some organizations, in others they are often misleading in their description of the reality of the workplace – its vision, norms, actors, events and interactions. In most companies, informal groups based on social networks and communities of practice are better indicators of company culture and the future potential of the organization. These 'shadow organizations' are often indicative of team competencies, organizational behaviour and a firm's capacity to change. What value is information technology in supporting formal organizational structures if it ignores or inhibits the development of informal social networks that bridge teams, departments and business communities? Perhaps the key to leveraging information technology in virtuous circles is to broaden the focus of our vision to take in the informal networks that may more accurately represent the organizations in which we work.

An organization's employees and managers can either foster or inhibit the organizational change that technological implementations target. These internal clients will alter their mindsets only if they see the point of the change and agree with it (at least up to a point). The technological and organizational structures (reflected in reward and recognition systems, for example) must be designed to measure and foster the desired outcomes. Managers and employees must be adequately trained to meet the challenges that change requires. Finally, each internal client must be able to see people they respect modelling it actively. Each of these conditions is independent of the others; but together they add up to a way of changing the behaviour of people in organizations by changing attitudes about what can and should happen at work (Lawson and Price, 2003).

Deploying information technology to support the informal networks of an effective organization requires rethinking IT investments on several levels. To begin with, different types of technology need to be developed to focus on people rather than on functions or processes. Next, analyze how information infrastructure supports knowledge transfer, decision making and the management of geographically dispersed teams. Further, measure not just the efficiency of formal structures, but notions of wisdom, creativity and innovation that characterize and feed social interaction and client relationships on all levels. Finally, think through the role of management: command and control needs to give way to new forms of leadership in building an effective organization.

What Have We Learned?

In this chapter we have examined the role of information technology in facilitating change in individuals, firms and markets. We have argued that 'productivity' depends not only on how we measure performance but on the information technology we use to do so. We have suggested three strategies for reconciling human endeavour, modern organizations and the market. One school of thought suggests strategies for influencing how we work by describing relevant 'skill sets' and relevant training strategies.

A second school argues that managers must introduce new 'mindsets' concerning the workplace before employees will accept that they have to change their skill sets. A third school argues that mindsets depend upon deeper-rooted collective beliefs about company culture, and that change management strategies need to begin by addressing the vision of what the company represents and how it wishes to develop. We have suggested that the Business Value Matrix™ can help you identify both the factors that contribute to successful implementations of technology, and the circumstances that tend to undermine these value propositions.

References

European Commission (2000) e-Learning – designing tomorrow's education, Communication from the Commission, Brussels, 16 May.

Fletcher, Richard (2004) Morrison starts by converting staff, *The Sunday Times*, 22 August.

Lawson, Emily, and Colin Price (2003) The psychology of change management, *The McKinsey Quarterly*, Special Edition: Organization.

Manyika, James M., and T. Michael Nevens (2002) Technology after the bubble, *The McKinsey Quarterly*, Number 4, Technology.

Schein, Edgar (1992) *Organizational Culture and Leadership*, 2nd edn, San Francisco: Jossey-Bass.

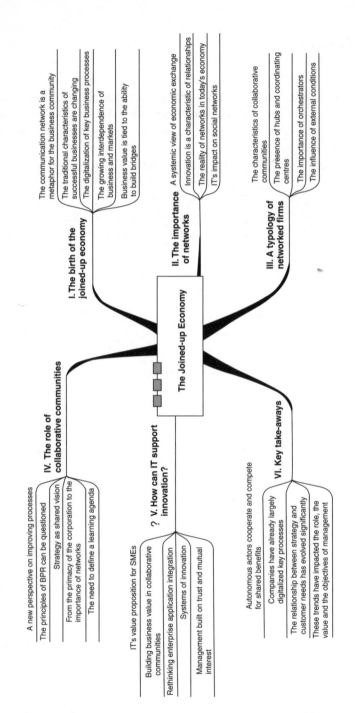

The Joined-up Economy

I. The birth of the joined-up economy
- The communication network is a metaphor for the business community
- The traditional characteristics of successful businesses are changing
- The digitalization of key business processes
- The growing interdependence of business and markets
- Business value is tied to the ability to build bridges

II. The importance of networks
- A systemic view of economic exchange
- Innovation is a characteristic of relationships
- The reality of networks in today's economy
- IT's impact on social networks

III. A typology of networked firms
- The characteristics of collaborative communities
- The presence of hubs and coordinating centres
- The importance of orchestrators
- The influence of external conditions

IV. The role of collaborative communities
- A new perspective on improving processes
- The principles of BPR can be questioned
- Strategy as shared vision
- From the primacy of the corporation to the importance of networks
- The need to define a learning agenda

V. How can IT support innovation?
- IT's value proposition for SMEs
- Building business value in collaborative communities
- Rethinking enterprise application integration
- Systems of innovation
- Management built on trust and mutual interest

VI. Key take-aways
- Autonomous actors cooperate and compete for shared benefits
- Companies have already largely digitalized key processes
- The relationship between strategy and customer needs has evolved significantly
- These trends have impacted the role, the value and the objectives of management

6
The Joined-up Economy

I was taking a short stroll late one evening beside Lake Maggiore in Stresa, Italy. The moonlight highlighted the beauty of the nineteenth-century architecture of the hotels, mansions, lakeside walks and lamp-posts. Caught up in the discussion of the moment, I had not noticed that I had dropped my hotel key somewhere along the way. As we doubled back looking for the key I was reminded of a story I had heard some years before. We habitually search for keys in the light of lamp-posts – even though we know the solutions to our problems lie somewhere further out in the dark.

A quick look at the headlines of the daily papers readily reveals a startling portrait of the traditional enterprise in the modern economy: it is struggling with increasingly diverse demands of employees, business partners and customers, with the globalization of economic activity, and with the increasing gap between the principles of traditional management and requirements of the networked economy. In taking a closer look at this living portrait, we could suggest that many corporations resemble modern-day 'Dorian Grays' – ageing dandies trying to prove their vitality in front of customers, business partners and shareholders with unprecedented amounts of information as proof of their value propositions.

In addressing the *joined-up economy*, we are suggesting a new vision for driving business value. The initial requirement is for a common understanding of business value, of how value is created in today's economy, and of how it can be enhanced in the future. To begin the discussion, we will explore how the association of strategy and customer needs puts pressure on the firm to unleash information resources. We will examine how the evolution of this relationship has impacted learning communities within the company and between the firm and its external clients. We will then analyze how the digitalization of key business processes has impacted the objectives and the structure of technology investments. We will conclude by suggesting that these trends have also impacted the role, the value and the objectives of management in supporting innovation.

Adapting information technology to the joined-up economy requires more than offering a web access to enterprise systems. To better understand how information technology can be leveraged in today's economy, we can raise a number of questions for discussion and debate:

- How can information technology adapt to add value in the joined-up economy?
- What role should business partners and customers play in defining the depth and the breadth of information resources?
- Who should determine IS strategies, and how can IS policy be driven across organizations?
- How are information technology projects financed for a business community, and how can commitment be ensured to maintain and grow the infrastructure across firms and industries?

The Birth of the Joined-up Economy

The reality of the joined-up economy is intimately tied to the development and the use of the Internet itself. The technical infrastructure of the communication network has become a metaphor for both markets and economies: 'decentralized', 'agile', 'connected', 'digitalized' are keywords of the modern enterprise. Following the bursting of the Internet bubble, what has really changed in the way corporations work internally and with their business environment? Has anything really changed in how we do business today?

Box 6.1: The joined-up economy

Although mixed economies have been prevalent in many countries to some degree for the last several decades, today's markets seem to reflect a *joined-up economy* in which autonomous actors at all levels cooperate and compete for shared benefits. More than just a 'networked economy', the joined-up economy differs in its organization, in its boundaries and in the nature of its interactions – decentralized, agile and connected, this complex web of relationships between public and private managers ties local markets firmly into a global economy. These social networks have bred a certain degree of consensus between government and market forces on a large number of economic, environmental and social objectives. Understanding the breadth and the depth of these social networks is critical to the understanding of the potential and the limits of challenges as diverse as corporate governance, shared service delivery and public support for the development of information technologies.

Traditionally, successful businesses have shared several defining characteristics. They have designed, manufactured and/or distributed products and services that met their client needs. The very internal organization of the company offered a source of competitive advantage. The physical organization of a company's product or service offer provided a basis for sustainable revenue streams. The role of information technology was limited to supporting internal business processes.

Strategy has traditionally been elaborated for companies that compete for resources in national and international markets. Implicit in this vision was the view of the firm as a coherent economic actor.[1] Strategy was viewed as a mechanistic response to corporate objectives and market imperatives. Decision-makers were free to shape their economic environments. All other factors being equal, a wise use of capital determined market success.

The industrial firm was perfected around specific functions such as marketing, sales, logistics and administration. The boundaries that separated the firm from clients and its competition were clearly defined financially, geographically and strategically. Innovation was guarded jealously at the heart of the enterprise, and was seen as a core element in competitive advance. Finally, improving processes were modelled in terms of efficiency: 'better' meant deploying human and physical resources to go quicker and less expensively to market.

In the last decade, innovative business executives have transformed their firms into networked businesses characterized by the 'digitalization' of key business processes, the establishment of market standards for information exchange, the development of business communities around concerns of shared benefits, and the co-engineering of new market opportunities.

The practice of management in today's economy has taken on new challenges. The vision of the firm as a coherent economic actor has been put to the question through outsourcing, partnering and streamlining the corporation into separate businesses of innovation, infrastructure and client relationship management. Corporate growth is no longer viewed as mechanistic, but as organic responses to stimuli within the firm and within business communities (see Rothwell *et al.*, 2002). All other factors being equal, an innovative use of talent determines market success (see Martin and Moldoveanu, 2003).

The growing interdependence of national economies has created an increasing number of players capable of providing the physical resources, capital and service needed to compete locally in any industry. At the same time, these forces have raised the pressure to unbundle the corporation into separate, more coherent units centred around core businesses of innovation, infrastructure and client relationship management (see Hagel and Singer, 1999). As a result, supply chains and business communities have become important economic forces in their own right. This situation calls for a common understanding of business value across business units, structures and communities.

The distinction between industrial and commercial concerns does not hold up for many companies today, no more than the functional distinctions between marketing, sales and customer service. The boundaries between firms and their markets are also becoming increasingly permeable as products and services are co-engineered, co-delivered and co-serviced by suppliers, distributors and their clients. Innovation is no longer seen as a characteristic of either products or services, but of human relationships between partners in a business community.

Box 6.2: The wealth of nations

Alan Warms, the CEO of Participate Systems, opens his story with a reference to Adam Smith's account of a pin factory in *The*

Wealth of Nations (1776) (Warms, 2003). In this factory, every worker performed all the steps necessary to produce a pin, the output of the factory being the sum of the pins produced by each worker. Smith proposed that, instead of working independently, each worker should be assigned a specialized task. The result would be an economy of scale, which could vastly increase the production of pins.

Whereas this concept of a division of labour played a major role in the Industrial Revolution, it can constitute a major hurdle in the networked economy. Interaction costs associated with the exchange of information, services and products increase as organizations grow, both internally and within their markets. The cost of interaction (locating, structuring and communicating information and experience within and between organizations) has become a real barrier to innovation and growth. Rather than proposing a division of labour, consultants like Alan Warms suggest just the opposite: economies of scale are derived today from sharing responsibility, conversation and vision.

In the future, business value will be tied to our ability to build bridges both between our organization and its market and between current practice and our vision of tomorrow. Much more than a networked economy, today's markets seem to reflect a *joined-up economy* in which autonomous actors at all levels cooperate and compete for shared benefits. Value in the joined-up economy will come from new learning paradigms for measuring IT performance and purpose.

The argument goes beyond simply redefining the relationship between economic actors in a given market. At its simplest level, the joined-up economy is about two things: almost instantaneous information exchange and almost unlimited 'connectedness'. The interactions between private and public concerns have become increasingly inter-dependent. Public intervention in the private sector has also been present; nonetheless, the nature and the depths of interrelationships today call out for a redefinition of how we view economic exchange.

On the one hand, the local economy is increasingly open to pressures from regional, national and international economic and political actors. On the other hand, public actors (associative, national and international) define, finance and regulate the core industries of the information economy (computer, telecoms, audio-visual etc.). Future strategic visions will be built upon new partnerships between public and private actors in service localities, supply chains and horizontal marketplaces. Improving processes in the future may mean focusing on effectiveness more than on efficiency: 'better' processes will improve the quality of interactions between internal and external clients.

Table 6.1 Traditional and joined-up economies

Characteristic	Traditional	Joined-up
Organization	Rigid	Organic
Components	Functions	Relationships
Boundaries	Hermetic	Permeable
Value levers	Improving process	Improving meaning
Primary metrics	Efficiency	Effectiveness
Innovation	In the core	On the edge

The Importance of Networks

If the joined-up economy involves more than just a marketing platform designed to sell information technology, what are the consequences for how we view the role of the firm and how we do business?

How does this paradigm influence how we structure processes to deliver products and services to our clients? What does this mean for commonly accepted forms of partnerships such as distribution and the supply chain? What will we need to learn to compete and to prosper in the joined-up economy?

The joined-up economy requires a systemic view of economic exchange. Rather than concentrating on economic actors themselves – employees, managers and organizations – independently, let us give priority to our analysis of the relationships between the different actors. We will suggest that economic networks are composed of human and physical resources that work towards common goals. The vitality of markets depends as much upon the presence of physical resources (raw materials, semi-finished and finished products) as it does upon the people who invent, design, distribute and consume them.

Economic activity cannot be separated from labour and organization. No matter where we focus on the product cycle – fundamental research, innovation, production or diffusion – economic activity is closely tied to our deeply embedded beliefs about the nature of business value, and also to how we structure social and economic networks (see Donkers, 2001). Innovation is not a characteristic of a product or service, but is inherent in how we organize the relationships between physical and human resources in firms, markets and the economy.

From this point of view, the firm is not the indivisible building block of the economy: organizations are complex mirrors of capital, physical resources and talent. If we accept this basic premise, we need to reconsider how we think about productivity. As a consequence, we can change our attitude to how we build value, and to the possibilities accompanying the emergence of change in organizations.

What are the realities of networks in today's economy? On the surface, it appears that the Internet has facilitated three types of structures. Observers note that the web has greatly improved economic exchanges between businesses. By the same token, they note that electronic exchanges have progressed, in small measure, in exchanges between businesses and consumers, or B2C. Electronic commerce sites, Internet banking and Internet auctions are examples of B2C. Finally, behind the notion of electronic government lies a third type of network: business to administration, or B2A. The use of the Internet by government agencies to improve purchasing and procurement policies is an example of this third type of network.

One consideration that merits attention is the extent to which technology has changed the basic form of networks. Exchanges between businesses, consumers and administrations went on long before the Internet came on the scene. The great majority of transactions continue to be managed today without the use of electronic exchanges. In instances where the Internet has had a measurable impact on commerce, for example in the banking or travel industries, the extent to which the web has changed the way people conduct transactions is still open to question. In spite of all the talk of new Internet business models, business models are still based on how processes are structured to produce products or services that meet client demands.

Another consideration is the extent to which these networks can be formalized. Has the advent of Internet technologies in fact led to the formulation of distinct digital networks between consumers, commerce and administration? To what degree can we talk about digital networks when the majority of exchanges involve a certain degree of human interaction? To what extent can we focus on separate networks, when in reality each is highly dependent upon the others? Similarly, can we improve any one network (for example, focusing on

B2B) without taking into account the corresponding consequences on other networks? Finally, is the formalization of separate and linear networks the most appropriate mindset to focus our attention on innovation and business value? What does 'better' mean?

A Typology of Networked Firms

What characteristics help to define collaborative communities in the joined-up economy? Several defining traits are characteristic of networked companies. The search for value brings and holds the community together; new opportunities are tested and exploited together. Such communities have defined a shared vision of standards of performance for their members. Similar standards exist concerning the nature and the form of information that needs to flow among community members. Benefits are distributed to varying degrees within the community. Business processes are structured both physically and digitally through the community as a whole.

Häcki and Lighton (2001) have distinguished distinct types of structures of such networked companies: community, value chains and knowledge services. Community structures are characteristic of networks that seek to promote open exchange of products and services throughout a given community. Cnet, e-Bay and Vindigo are examples of community structures. Important to how the community is structured are 'hubs' – which Henry Mintzberg describes as 'coordinating centres' where people, things or information move (Mintzberg and van der Heyden, 1999).

Value chains are a second type of network structure, defined by the need to ensure effective design of the product or service offer to a given group of companies. Cisco and Palm are offered as examples of value chain networks. Finally, knowledge services networks are structured to better organize a portfolio of services among partners serving a common set of customers. Charles Schwab and e-Trade are example of knowledge services networks in which the organization's core competency is that of orchestrating their business community.[2]

Each of these types of structure differs in the importance given either to one company as the central orchestrator of the community or, in contrast, to individual partners or cells. Community networks allow the operational boundaries of the network to be defined by the customers, whereas a central orchestrator plays a fundamental role in determining community limits in value chains or knowledge services communities. Individual partners are largely given a free rein in community networks, whereas partners co-manage value chains, and orchestrators determine the rules of adhesion in knowledge services networks.

Häcki and Lighton (2001) go on to argue that such networked structures have demonstrated their ability to build business value regardless of external conditions. The authors are less demonstrative as to whether the networks are universally applicable or whether they are conditioned by the nature of certain industries (information technology, information services and knowledge services). The vision and role of individual companies (other than the orchestrator) is also left unexplored. To what extent is collaboration a result of individual strengths or weaknesses? Equally unclear is the impact of the external environment on the community. To what extent are community networks influenced by government regulations and civic culture, and to what extent are they products of a given economic system?

The Role of Collaborative Communities

The emergence of the joined-up economy requires us to take a fresh look at how we structure processes as well as at what we are trying to improve. Business process improvement traditionally makes a number of assumptions concerning the nature of business processes. Processes have been defined as linear sets of internal activities and tasks. These activities transform intermediate resources into products or services that best meet their clients' needs. Improving processes means reducing the transaction costs inherent in and between these activities.

The joined-up economy puts to the test some of these hypotheses. To begin with, we assume that processes are not embedded in any one company, but most often bridge companies in social networks or collaborative communities.[3] The shared activities and tasks involve not only transaction costs but interaction costs associated with allocating resources between economic actors in any given market. Improving processes in a joined-up economy means not just saving time and money but focusing attention on how activities can be structured to scale economies across supply chains, business communities and economies as a whole. Innovation takes on new meaning: it is not embedded in any one product or service, but in relationships on the edges of organizations in their interactions with other economic actors.

By their very nature, collaborative communities differ fundamentally from the corporate enterprise. Strategy is not the result of a corporate mission statement but of a shared vision that has been developed within a given business community. Leadership is not reserved to a board of directors but orchestrated among more or less independent actors. The boundaries and roles of economic actors are not predetermined functions, but are negotiated within the community itself. Finally, the reality of the market is even less dependent upon formal models than the corporation: the life of the community is an informal web of human interaction.

Given the shift from the primacy of the corporation to the importance of networking, what exactly do we need to learn to compete and to prosper in the joined-up economy? What learning objectives can and should be set by individual firms for their employees, managers and business partners? To what extent will internal organizational constraints impact individuals' opportunities to learn? What role can information technology play in facilitating or limiting the learning agenda?

The learning agenda can be set at various levels for each consumer, employee and manager. At the base, we can suggest that learning involves the transfer of information from one actor to another. A higher level would complement this simple information transfer by developing an individual's (or an organization's) specific knowledge or skill set. A third level builds on the first two in creating new skills or knowledge in meeting specific market demands. Finally, a fourth-level learning objective is for economic actors to be able to dynamically develop their competencies in response to changing market demands and objectives.

A manager's ability to learn is influenced by how the organization structures learning opportunities. In organizations characterized by hierarchical control, information flows in one direction from management to employees. In employee-centred structures, the learning agenda is determined by the employee's needs and objectives. In team-centred, flat organizations, the agenda is determined by interactions

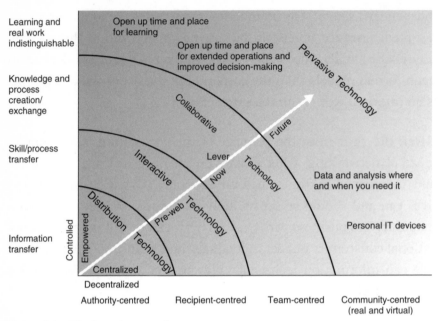

Figure 6.1 The learning agenda
Source: Dr Richard Straub

of internal clients attempting to deal with market challenges. Finally, in the joined-up economy, the learning agenda is determined not by the organization but by the nature of its interactions within a collaborative community.

How can information technology support these learning agendas? Almost any information technology can facilitate the flow of data from top to bottom in hierarchical organizations. However, there is little that any information technology can do to overcome the handicap of hierarchical structures when choosing more ambitious learning agendas. Information technology can only serve as a mirror reflecting the coherence of organizational structures with market needs. If we accept that higher-level learning objectives are more appropriate than information transfer in a joined-up economy, modelling organizational structures to mirror the learning agenda is a prerequisite for the effective application of IT.

How Can IT Support Innovation in the Joined-up Economy?

How does applying information technology to core processes improve business? Can the principles of business process improvement be applied as easily to small businesses as to large corporations? Can these principles, which were designed to improve internal processes, be applied successfully to processes that span several firms or even communities?

Classically, information technology has been applied in understanding, designing and restructuring business processes. Improvement has been achieved in several areas. To begin with, the use of information technology can provide better or more complete information on how specific activities and tasks contribute to the production of targeted products or services. On a different level, information technology can pinpoint obstacles and bottlenecks in existing processes that hamper production or service delivery. Information technology can sometimes replace physical activities, and at substantial cost savings. Alternatively, information technology can be applied to redesigning the routing of process activities.

The application of IT to business processes in small firms needs to be handled with caution. Many SMEs are characterized by rigid hierarchical forms of 'leadership'. Information flows from top to bottom. Business-to-business relationships are seen as conflicting rather than consensual, win–lose rather than win–win. Another key characteristic of this 'sector' is that most firms do not possess several of the core processes (development, manufacturing, sales, delivery, after-sales service) normally associated with 'doing business'. The vast majority of small businesses have little room to manoeuvre: they are not acting at the 'centre' of their markets, but reacting on the periphery to client demands.

Successfully building business value in collaborative communities requires a common vision concerning both the way one does business and how one structures information architectures. In the past, people saw business as a 'winner takes all' or 'zero-sum' game. The joined-up economy moves away from these purely competitive plays to recognize cooperative relationships that leverage value created by those in the network. A new paradigm has evolved where information, connectivity and time define how business is conducted. Information is richer in quality and quantity, promoting collaboration among players. Connectivity, in particular via the Internet, has also lowered barriers to entry and bred hyper-competition on a global scale. And time is increasingly a critical, and scarce, resource.

The widespread adoption of the Internet and mobile technologies have made it even more necessary for companies to both cooperate and compete in capturing, structuring and communicating data, information and, eventually, market knowledge.[4] Integrating information resources within collaborative communities requires rethinking enterprise application integration (EAI) at several levels. To begin with, companies within a business community can focus on a common definition of business processes through workflow modelling. The next step involves platform integration to ensure that the information infrastructure is capable of transporting data across the network.

A further step is the application integration needed so that data can be located and processed regardless of the constraints of particular applications or programs. Finally, a fourth level involves data integration and developing tools to extract, transform and load data.

How Does Management Support Innovation in the Networked Economy?

Innovation is a gradual and accumulative phenomenon. W. E. Deming pointed out that future innovation is dependent both on the current context and on the past. In any given market, innovation is the potential fruit of interactions between individuals, firms and institutions. Schumpeter (1934) suggested, in his theory of economic development, that entrepreneurs were primarily responsible for introducing innovation to an economic system. He later revised his theoretical scheme and suggested that innovation depended less on the entrepreneur than on teams specializing in R&D (Schumpeter, 1942). Were he writing today, Schumpeter might suggest that the innovation process is synonymous with cooperation in supply chains and social networks.

Box 6.3: **Managers could probably learn a lot from a Lego® set**

In listening to my management students explain the structure and objectives of their professional projects, I often end up thinking about playing with the pieces in a Lego box. The value of the pieces is not in their size, their colour, or their number, but in the imagination of those who use the pieces to

---

build their vision. The Lego experience is based upon playing, learning, interacting, exploring, expressing, discovering, creating and imagining. As a corporation, Lego has built its brand not on its product offer or its reputation but on 'the relationship a person has with our company through products and services'. Managers could probably learn a lot from Lego: the value of their projects is not in the intelligence of their own ideas, nor in the quantity of resources available, but in how the project will allow their clients to piece together future visions.

What are the building blocks of a successful management project in the joined-up economy? If the context is defined by a constantly evolving environment, the absence of one best way, and the search for answers to problems that may not even exist today, what is the shape, colour and number of required blocks? Client loyalty, customer acquisition, ubiquitous communication and continuous feedback remain fundamental objectives. The value of technology and organization is directly dependent on their contribution to achieving these objectives. As with the Lego set, project success for a manager in the joined-up economy is tied to offering the pieces necessary to enable their clients' visions to emerge.

Systems of innovation are now viewed as prerequisites for survival in the networked economy. Lundvall refers to a 'national system of innovation' which includes all actors and aspects of the economic structure: the production, marketing and finance systems are subsystems in which learning takes place. Such activities include learning-by-doing, increasing the efficiency of production operations, learning-by-using, increasing the efficiency of the use of complex systems, and learning-by-interacting, in which innovation is a potential by-product of collaboration between economic agents (Lundvall and Johnson, 1992).

Innovation is not confined solely within the economic arena; innovation is the result of interactions between social, economic and political agents. Wilson (2003) suggests innovation to social exchanges within Quad partnerships. A Quad is a social network of sustained interactions among leaders in complementary sectors – government officials, private managers and entrepreneurs, researchers, and leaders in civil society (associations). Although each of these actors has his or her own particular interests and perspectives, they seek common solutions to business problems that span the social, political and economic arenas.

In this joined-up economy, the manager has several options for action, whether it is the local entrepreneur in her start-up firm, the line manager or the lead researcher in a laboratory. One option is to motivate and organize people within our own sector. A second is to reach out beyond our management teams to engage with others. A third is to build shared vision that can serve as a catalyst for collaboration. Finally, management in the networked economy is built upon sustained and regular exchanges built on trust and mutual interest.

What does a manager need to learn to contribute in a joined-up economy? Before we address this question in more detail in the next chapter, consider a few key questions:

- Who are the players in your network and how can they collaborate to maximize value?
- Which relationships are complementary in nature – which companies can they work with that can add value to what they provide?

- Which players are competitors, and are there mutually beneficial ways to create value?
- What can you do to leverage relationships with customers and suppliers?
- What can you do to sustain competitive advantage over time?

What Have We Learned?

In this chapter we have addressed a *joined-up economy* in which autonomous actors at all levels cooperate and compete for shared benefits. The emergence of the joined-up economy requires a fresh look at what we are trying to improve and how we structure our business processes across collaborative communities. We have examined how the evolving relationship between strategy and customer needs has impacted learning communities within the company and between the firm and its external clients. Our premise pleads for a common understanding of business value, of how value is created in today's economy, and how it can be enhanced in future.

An increasing number of players are capable of providing the physical resources, capital and services needed to compete locally in any industry. The vision of a firm as a coherent economic actor is strongly challenged by the reality of outsourcing, partnering and 'unbundling' the corporation into separate businesses of innovation, infrastructure and client relationship management. We have analysed how the digitalization of key business processes impacts the objectives and the structure of technology investments. We conclude by suggesting that these trends have also impacted the role, the value and the objectives of management itself in fostering the creation of business value.

Notes

1. In what they have called a 'network theory', Latour and Callon (Latour, 1999) developed a vocabulary around 'actors' and 'actants' that takes into account the relationships between subjects and objects. In economic networks, employees (actors), organizations and technology (actants) impact and are impacted by each other; i.e. matter matters. For the purposes of this chapter, we refer only to the concept of 'actors'. For a more developed analysis, see Law and Hassard (1999).
2. John Seely Brown, Scott Durschlag and John Hagel III define orchestrators as companies that recruit other organizations 'into a process network, structure appropriate incentives for participants; encourage increasing specialization over time, define standards for communication, coordination, dynamically create tailored business processes, assume ultimate responsibility for the end products or services, develop and manage performance feedback loops, and cultivate deep understanding of processes and practices to improve quality, speed, cost-competitiveness of the network ...'. See Brown *et al.* (2002).
3. A social network can be defined by the connections among a group of social actors. These links or relationships are defined and maintained by persistent, repeated actions between the actors. Although the concepts are somewhat interchangeable, we prefer the term 'collaborative community' to focus attention both on the interactions rather than the actors, and on the will to collaborate as the glue that holds the community together.
4. Brandenburger and Nalebuff suggest that businesses can gain advantage by means of a judicious mixture of competition and cooperation. Cooperation with suppliers, customers and firms producing complementary or related products can lead to expansion of the market and the formation of new business relationships, perhaps even the creation of new forms of enterprise. See Brandenburger and Nalebuff (1996).

References

Brandenburger, Adam J., and Barry J. Nalebuff (1996) *Co-opetition*, New York: Currency Doubleday.

Brown, John Seely, Scott Durschlag and John Hagel III (2002) Loosening up: how process networks unlock the power of specialization, *The McKinsey Quarterly*, Special Edition: Risk and Resilience.

Donkers, H. W. J. (2001) Technological change and innovation in a networked economy, Paper prepared for the ECIS Conference: The Future of Innovation Studies, 20–23 September, 2001.

Häcki, Remo, and Julian Lighton (2001) The future of the networked company, *The McKinsey Quarterly*, Number 3.

Hagel, John III, and Marc Singer (1999) Unbundling the corporation, *Harvard Business Review*, March–April.

Latour, Bruno (1999) On recalling ANT. In Law and Hassard (1999).

Law, John, and Hassard, John (Editors) (1999) *Actor Network Theory and After*, Oxford: Blackwell.

Lundvall, Bengt-Åke, and B. Johnson (1994) The learning economy, *Journal of Industry Studies*, Vol. 1, Iss. 2, 23–42.

Martin, Roger, and Mihnea C. Moldoveanu (2003) Capital versus talent: the battle that's reshaping business, *Harvard Business Review*, 1 July.

Mintzberg, Henry, and L. van der Heyden (1999) Organigraphs: drawing how companies really work, *Harvard Business Review*, September–October.

Rothwell *et al.* (2002) In Stan Herman (Editor), *Rewiring Organizations for the Networked Economy*, San Francisco: Jossey-Bass.

Schumpeter, Joseph A. (1934) *The Theory of Economic Development*, Cambridge, MA: Harvard University Press. (New York: Oxford University Press, 1961.) First published in German, 1912.

Schumpeter, Joseph A. (1942) *Capitalism, Socialism, and Democracy*, New York: Harper & Brothers.

Warms, Alan (2003) Online community: a new paradigm for achieving economies of scale. (http://community.capgemini.com/focus/articles/InsightArticleIssue14a.pdf.)

Wilson, Ernest J. (2003) Leadership for a networked world, Presented at the ICT Development Forum, Petersberg, Germany.

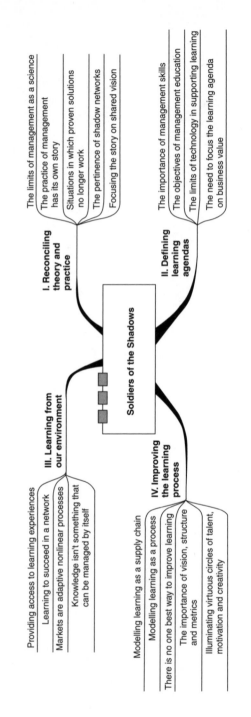

Soldiers of the Shadows

I. Reconciling theory and practice
- The limits of management as a science
- The practice of management has its own story
- Situations in which proven solutions no longer work
- The pertinence of shadow networks
- Focusing the story on shared vision

II. Defining learning agendas
- The importance of management skills
- The objectives of management education
- The limits of technology in supporting learning
- The need to focus the learning agenda on business value

III. Learning from our environment
- Providing access to learning experiences
- Learning to succeed in a network
- Markets are adaptive nonlinear processes
- Knowledge isn't something that can be managed by itself

IV. Improving the learning process
- Modelling learning as a supply chain
- Modelling learning as a process
- There is no one best way to improve learning
- The importance of vision, structure and metrics
- Illuminating virtuous circles of talent, motivation and creativity

7
Soldiers of the Shadows

*P*hilippe warmly anticipated the opportunity to contribute to his bank's new management education programme. This seasoned IT professional strongly supported the new Managing Director's vision to leverage information technology to breed a new corporate culture into the organization. This 200-year-old French bank was firmly committed to bringing in new blood, and an innovative training agenda could provide the motivation to carry this venerable institution into the coming century. Most of the old guard had already left the firm; those that stayed on would need to adapt to the needs of the market or face early retirement. Upon the belief that training should be a protected source of competitive advantage, Philippe took particular care in building a secure and robust information architecture. The Managing Director's first question when reviewing the project was: When will the system be available to clients, partners and stakeholders?

Several themes are woven into the pages that follow. Management education is embedded in business and the business community rather than being packaged in a course or a degree. The value of education of managers is not in identifying high-level models of what employees need to do, but in bringing each employee closer to his or her personal and professional goals. Leveraging learning is about using information technology to break down the physical and mental barriers between 'learning' and 'work', rather than pushing learning out of the workplace or promoting quicker and cheaper training strategies. Finally, building a successful learning community implies designing learning strategies that complement individual needs and company culture.

Within this context, let us begin by exploring the challenges of learning 'modern' principles of management. On the one hand, we can examine the current relevance of the traditional paradigm of management. On the other hand, we can investigate the coherence of individual needs and objectives. We can conclude by examining how companies can reframe the learning agenda to build a more effective organization.

- What do we need to learn to be successful in the 'effective organization'?
- What objectives do companies set for corporate education?
- What does a manager have to know?
- How can information technology support this learning process?

Reconciling Theory and Practice

Management theory has been traditionally focused on proposing models of power, leadership and organizational boundaries. The hierarchical control, functional definitions of work, and empiricism outlined by Frederic Taylor at the beginning of the twentieth century continue to characterize the prescriptions of 'modern' management. As Drucker (1998) lamented, traditional management is essentially telling workers what they need to do. Embedded in this vision is a conception of leadership based on the ubiquity of company culture, the stability of market needs, and the principle of 'one best way'.

Management itself is viewed as a science: organizational behaviour, whether inside the firm or across the market, is predictable, understandable and quantifiable. Bred into the bone of management science is the belief that there are simple, empirical answers to corporate success, no matter what the business challenge. Management drives a charted course of change through the company by *unfreezing* or contesting operational practice, *moving* to a new vision of organizational performance, and then *refreezing* this new basis of corporate productivity (Lewin, 1951). In this light, the manager's job is one of command and control: he or she sets the boundaries for acceptable company culture, organizational behavior and efficiency.

The practice of management has brought to light a quite different story of the employee, the firm and the market. The perceived stability of the firm and its market is an illusion; complexity or even chaos are probably more accurate descriptions of the environments in which most of us work. Employee behaviour is as difficult to quantify as it is to measure; employees themselves are often incapable of explaining exactly what they do. In such a context, it is very presumptuous to believe that managers have developed the gift of knowing what the future holds. Rather than driving change through the organization, new methods of management must be developed to help employees understand and adapt to a constantly changing business environment.

Taken as a whole, the complexity of organizational dynamics renders long-term planning haphazard at best. Formal organizational structures are of little help in understanding how work is actually performed; social or shadow networks are better indicators of why certain individuals, teams and companies outperform their competition. In focusing on human capital (practical knowledge, acquired skills and learned abilities), training schemes undervalue the specific benefits that flow from the trust, reciprocity, information and cooperation associated with social capital. As a result, management often views strategic plans as exercises in marketing. This gap between models of management and the reality of the market has marked the workforce with anxiety, cynicism and disillusionment.

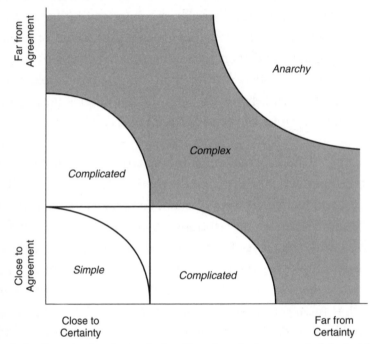

Figure 7.1 Organizational complexity. How does the human mind deal with instability, complexity and emotion?
Source: Ralph Stacy (1995) *Strategic Management and Organisational Dynamics*, Hemel Hempstead: Prentice Hall. By permission of Pearson Education Ltd.

Why does this gap exist, and why does workforce antipathy to management seem to increase as the years go by? Rather than looking for the solution engraved in stone (or even in this book), take a moment to reflect on how you solve real-life business challenges. How does the human mind deal with instability, complexity and emotion? How do we deal with situations in which 'proven' solutions no longer seem to work?[1]

Box 7.1: Soldiers of the shadows

One of the most discussed stories of all time is 'The Allegory of the Cave' in Book VII of Plato's *The Republic*. As the story unfolds, a group of people are chained to the wall of a metaphorical cavern. Behind the prisoners a fire burns, but all that they can see are shadows on the wall, all they can hear are echoes of the enlightened people walking and talking behind them. At one point in time, one of prisoners is freed of his chains, and leaves the cave to adapt to the real world. He is challenged to decide how to lead his former companions out of the shadows and into the light of new knowledge. Traditionally, training is modelled as a confined and ordered world in which one leads and the others follow, in which there are right answers and acceptable behaviour, in which the evaluation criteria have stood the test of time.

This well-structured learning-place contrasts sharply with the world around us: in our jobs, our careers and our business communities we are increasingly burdened with chains of doubt, frustration and antipathy, and few if any know what their professional futures may hold. It is always easier to lead people into the light where there are proven answers and the obstacles are clearly identified. It is a much more difficult task to encourage people to venture into the dark where there are no universal solutions to the obstacles that are lurking in the shadows. Classical management theory sees senior management as generals leading well-disciplined armies of employees into battle (from the safety of their boardrooms) as dawn breaks each day. The practice of management in the global economy suggests a much murkier picture: management is about constantly searching for answers to client pain, employee apathy and declining margins by encouraging informal networks of collaborators, partners and clients to take the risk of venturing beyond the well-lit and well-travelled paths of their past experience. Training tomorrow's managers may focus less on producing knights in white armour and more on producing soldiers of the shadows.

Studies of synectics suggest that the mind is a dynamic, self-organizing system capable of proposing adaptive responses to new situations.[2] The mind does not store clear ideas of the 'right answers', but captures relationships of stimuli that can provide the 'best response' to challenges from the environment. Consequently, knowledge cannot be easily extracted from the context in which it emerged: structure and context are inherently entwined in our perceptions of knowledge and reality. The learning process is not so much about memorizing 'facts' as developing our capacity to detect patterns in external stimuli. This process is at the very heart of imagination and creative destruction.

With this in mind, we would like to focus our story on shared vision. Shared vision cannot be imposed upon us by company mission statements, clearly defined functions and command and control; but it can result from a common approach to understanding our business challenges, of exploring and discussing appropriate responses to building business value, and of fostering the emergence of organizational knowledge in the effective organization.

The pertinence of this practice of management will not be described precisely in an organizational chart or measured in formal organizational structures, but will be fostered in the uncharted areas of informal structures and social networks. Organization innovation and creativity is not conceived in board meetings or company conferences; it emerges from discussions in hallways and coffee rooms. In these conditions, how can managers become effective soldiers of these shadow organizations?

Defining Learning Agendas

How do we create globally competitive organizations capable of sustained effective performance in the joined-up economy? To date, corporate education has provided fewer answers than questions concerning what exactly managers need to learn to contribute to their organizations. What specific goals are set for educating managers? Is there a difference of view between corporations and small and medium-sized companies? What objectives are set for corporate training? What considerations are taken into account in designing training programmes? What is the role and value of technology in enhancing the training process? Although the debate is far from conclusive, several trends can be identified.

Does business value come from the quality of an organization's human resources? The conclusions of a recent study of Fortune 1000 companies seem to indicate that it does. Company interviews indicated that 70% of the CEOs cited the ability to attract and retain skilled employees as a major issue for growth and competitiveness. Contrastingly, the survey is less precise in defining management skills: the ability to sell and support multiple product lines, the ability to deliver accurate and consistent customer service, and the ability to comply with legal and regulatory mandates (Moe, 2000). Current discussion in corporate education revolves around how to develop these competencies and to what degree corporate training programmes can contribute.

Box 7.2: Promising not to be 'evil'

Larry Page and Sergey Brin have recently published 'An Owner's Manual' for Google's Shareholders, the organizational manifesto of the co-founders of this Internet search company. The seven-page text contradicts many of the traditional principles for operating a public corporation. The authors promise not to be 'evil' by sacrificing their ideals to short-term financial gains, and express a deep scepticism of the establishment financial community.

Although Google highly publicizes its freewheeling culture (which includes roller-blade hockey matches and free food cooked by the Grateful Dead's former chef), it may well be the company's commitment to innovation that sets it apart from its competition. Contractually, Google engineers are expected to spend one day a week on projects of personal interest unrelated to their assigned work. One of the immediate paybacks has been the invention of G-mail, which uses information technology to automatically identify and organize messages in the form and context of the original conversation.

The views of the managing directors of small and medium-sized businesses offer complementary and contrasting views. The Tomillo Foundation's study of training needs in European SMEs revealed that one-quarter to one-third of the owners of small businesses put competencies associated with quality, team building, customer service and change management at the top of their list for their training programmes. Nonetheless, the same study indicates that over half the sample felt that the primary objective for training was learning supervision techniques (command and control), and an even larger percentage felt that training should focus primarily on understanding information technology.[3] Do these figures indicate a correlation between small business and beliefs that value comes from process or technology rather than organization, or that training is more suited to teach hard skills than to foster softer organizational competencies?

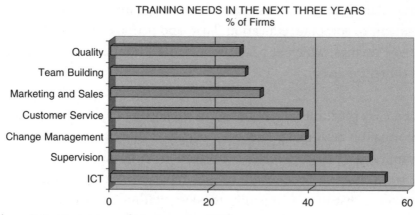

TRAINING NEEDS IN THE NEXT THREE YEARS
% of Firms

Figure 7.2   Training needs in European SMEs
Source: Tomillo Foundation.

Our own survey of European management education leaders concerning their objectives for corporate training completes this picture.[4] Of the 44 directors interviewed, the large majority felt that learning programmes needed to be integrated into the objectives and organization of the workplace. Almost as large a number felt that the learning programmes needed to be organizationally coherent with the culture and vision of the corporation. Next on the list was the notion of event-driven learning agendas: that learning content needs to be determined and structured around the patterns of interaction between managers and their internal and external clients. The personalization of 'course content' also received considerable mention, suggesting a link between content and the structure of social interaction. To what extent should managers be responsible for their own education?

What is technology's value proposition in corporate education? Technology can lead to anywhere, anytime access of learning content, and greatly improved access to tutors and knowledge bases. Technology can support attempts to standardize content and delivery leading to a more consistent approach to the learning process. Electronically capturing interactions between students and instructors can facilitate data analysis and enrich strategies of linking human resource management to corporate education. Last, and perhaps least, is the claim of cost savings, which at best can be derived from economies of scale in content delivery.

Where are the limits of technology in supporting the learning process? Information technology has been deployed more often to distribute technical data than to foster conversation on human, organizational or social issues. Technology cannot replace social interaction, and can often distort and magnify tensions within a learning community. Learning technologies are most often incapable of promoting knowledge transfer because of our inability to quantify and qualify the management context in which we work. IT is often deployed as a means of 'educating' more quickly and less expensively, where learning may be less a question of efficiency than of creativity, innovation and passion.

Box 7.3: And if business value was a question of places and passions?

Social geographers suggest that we divide our lives into three places: the work place, the family place, and a very personal 'third place'. Each place has its own vision, norms, actors, events, outcomes and even a gateway to the other places. Conflict

---

characterizes the work place, and to some degree the family place, for we define neither the vision, nor the actors, nor the outcomes. This may be one of reasons why it is that, while we are physically at work, we escape mentally several times a day into less stressful, more passionate places. The 'third place', on the other hand, is filled with passion: a good book or game for some, a memorable night in a pub for others, a place where we are/were kings for a day. Rather than deploy information technology to focus attention on the work at hand, consultants from the Doblin Group[6] suggest the real value of information technology is helping us escape temporarily to calmer waters, and to return to work refreshed with the passion of our 'third place'.

What management skills can be associated with management in a joined-up economy? If organizations offer little guidance about what we need to learn to survive and compete, what should individual managers learn to add value to their teams, companies and careers? How has the evolution of the modern economy affected what we need to learn? What do we need to learn about business value? Should our learning focus on production processes or those associated with the services and information embedded in the product offer? How can we venture into the shadows when there are no universal solutions?

Certain changes in the nature of markets and economies should be taken into account in determining what and how we learn about adding value. As we discussed previously, the primacy of markets based on factories producing physical goods has been challenged by networked companies relying on services and information to create sustainable competitive value. Specialization by trade and by function has been contested by those who advocate specialization by mega-processes of innovation, infrastructure and client relationship management. Information technology has moved from the periphery of the workplace to the centre in building and sustaining partnerships linked by omnipresent information networks.

Globalization has brought us flatter, more agile organizations, less dependent on local cultures and more sensitive to innovation and to the challenges of international markets. As a consequence of this constantly changing environment, once-only education has been contested by notions of lifelong learning: i.e. managers who stop learning are ready to retire. Finally, the focus of learning has grown from simply defining organizational agendas to exploring what individual managers need to know to add value to their teams, their organizations and their careers.

We have defined value as the essence of an organization's identity: why stakeholders (customers, employees, investors, suppliers, partners, etc.) choose to do business with that organization. As discussed previously, client perceptions today are defined largely by the services and information that are embedded around product offers. Managers' ability to add value to their teams and organizations is thus tied to their understanding of client needs and objectives, the costs and benefits of their activities, and the optimization of service supply chains between internal and external clients. Client needs themselves can be expressed in terms of either goal attainment, community building, or the assimilation of the attributes associated with the use of a company's products or services. If these areas of business are at the heart of propositions of added value, they, rather than traditional curricula of management education, should be at the core of the learning agenda.

Learning from Your Environment

On an individual level, we can infer by analogy that value is part of the essence of a manager's identity: why his or her colleagues, employees and clients choose to do work with him. Promoting organizational efficiency is an integral part of a manager's job at all levels of the organization. Fostering organizational effectiveness is a characteristic of successful managers whose teams get the job done. Organizational effectiveness is rooted in relationships and social networks within a business community. Relationships are owned by people within organizations and not by the organizations themselves. People make the difference with regard to establishing and maintaining relationships. People decide what they are willing to learn to compete and to succeed.

Organizational culture and context influence our ability to learn from our environment. The organization's vision, rules, 'instructors' and resources either favour or hinder each individual's ability to learn. The development of collaborative technologies suggests that information technology can play a role in reducing the cost of interacting with the environment. Such technologies can help overcome the challenges of distance, of time and of culture in reinforcing the proximity between the individuals and their learning agenda.

Since individual efforts do not necessarily contribute to better products and services, similar metrics can be developed to monitor and evaluate how teams, departments and organizations respond to client needs. Good management education needs to be tied no longer to companies that have hired the best trainers or purchased the best off-the-shelf courses, but to organizations that have provided the best access to learning experiences.

Box 7.4: Talent is the best investment of all

Mellon Global Investments is the tenth largest asset management company in the world. Marilyn, Senior Vice-President of the corporation, pointed out to me how the market's perceptions of business value have changed dramatically in recent years. Her fund managers are seriously challenged by increasingly direct access to multiple sources of information, more than ever before. Analysts use information technology to take a much closer look at what lies behind the figures and why companies perform the way they do. This is a double-edged sword, because clients also have greater access to their own information and more and more often draw their own conclusions on how their investments should be handled.

When Marilyn started her career in the industry, she felt that most of her colleagues could get by with a bit of flair and knowledge of the finance basics. She argues today that times have changed: market fund managers have to add value to their organizations on three levels: in running the funds themselves, in managing their client's expectations, and in aggregating client knowledge. She claims that her top people today need to have a unique combination of business knowledge, systems expertise, industry acumen and a deep understanding of client perspectives. She concludes that, in an industry burdened by information overflow, nurturing this kind of talent is the best investment of all.

Learning to succeed in a networked environment requires more than learning about making better processes and products. The cost of doing business in the joined-up economy is not limited to the physical costs of largely autonomous economic actors manufacturing products. Transaction costs, as previously discussed, include these costs related to the formal exchange of goods and services between companies or between companies and customers. Interaction costs include not only those costs but also the costs of exchanging ideas and information between economic actors in a joined-up economy.[5] Learning to recognize what reduces interaction costs between individuals, project teams and companies is a vital component of the learning agenda (Hagel and Singer, 1999).

In sharp contrast to the prescription of 'one best way' inherent in the efficiency paradigm, there is no crystal ball for predicting the course of action in the effective organization. The very complexity of the organization and the market, in stark contrast to the immobility and the simplicity of process models, suggests a different course of action. Organizations and markets are social systems that can best be described as adaptive nonlinear processes. Much like the human mind, the informal structures that characterize both are self-organizing systems.

If we accept this construct, there are several hypotheses that follow. Knowledge is not something that can be managed itself; knowledge is embedded in our social interactions. Rather than imposing command and control, management seeks negotiated consensus. Management is not about imposing a long-term vision so much as improving outcomes as individuals, teams and companies adapt to the specificities of their market. Learning is not so much about our ability to memorize appropriate answers as about our capability to understand how particular business challenges differ.

Improving the Learning Process

The learning process can be improved in any one of a number of ways. Learning can be modelled as a supply chain: a network of activities that assure the functions of procurement, transformation and distribution of applicable experience to a business community. In this light, managers can focus on the pertinence and the coherence of learning opportunities that reinforce individual and team competencies within the organization. We can improve the training by carefully monitoring the learning agenda, comparing demands with outcomes, and benchmarking the current offer across divisions, companies or markets. We can apply information technologies to better capture, store and communicate relevant data or information for internal and external clients of the organization.

Another set of opportunities exists in modelling learning as a process. Potential benefits are created by optimizing or redesigning individual learning activities: lower cost, better information, increased impact. Further benefits may be identified in broadening the scope of improvement to the learning process itself: increased visibility, coherence or reduced interaction costs. Other benefits may be derived from redesigning the place of learning with the organization by reframing the outcomes, redesigning the responsibilities, or modifying the physical resources dedicated to learning. New opportunities may be identified in the social relationships between the organization and its internal and external clients: co-marketing, partnering, and communities of practice. Finally, the learning agenda may provide new business opportunities: opening up new channels or markets, permitting 'mass personalization' of existing products, facilitating the conception of new products and services.

A further value proposition may be derived in improving the various activities associated with educating our managers. Information technologies can be used to improve organizational knowledge of individual skills and objectives, as well as employee profiling. Information technologies can be implemented to enrich content for educating managers by monitoring, capturing and storing data on how managers actually work. Information technologies can improve the delivery of training material by adapting the learning agenda to the constraints and opportunities of the workplace. Information technologies can evaluate the impact of the learning agenda by monitoring how successfully learning is applied to client challenges. Finally, technologies can support human resources management by facilitating schemes that reinforce positive learning.

There is no one best way to improve the learning agenda. Individual objectives, company culture and market requirements help to shape the learning objectives set by individual managers and the organization as a whole. For certain managers, learning may be limited to information transfer: getting the right information to the right people at the right time. For others, learning may be defined as actually developing the skills and knowledge of the workforce. For others still, learning objectives may be extended to facilitating the emergence of new skills and competencies. Finally, some organizations may aim to create learning organizations in which learning becomes second nature to the workforce.

Organizational structures do impact the ability of individual companies to reach learning objectives. Information transfer is typical of authority-centred organizations, in which a limited number of individuals decide and the vast majority execute. Moving beyond information transfer to other levels of learning objectives requires different organizational structures. Recipient-centred organizations are better suited to fostering skill and competency development. Team-centred organizations are better able to foster the social interactions associated with the development of new skills and knowledge. Finally, learning agendas designed around collaborative communities may well facilitate the association of learning and work.

A third set of opportunities can be constructed in focusing learning along the Business Value Matrix™. If a central prerequisite for adding value in a business community is the development of a shared vision of how to move forward, care should be taken in focusing management attention on the basics of value creation. Where do the organization's clients feel value come from: from the skills and competencies of the work force, from the optimization of organizational processes or from technological sophistication? How can the organization best respond to client pain: by working on individual performance and achievements, but improving collaboration between teams and organizations, or by bringing the clients closer to the organization? What are the primary metrics that clients are using to judge the organization: efficiency, profitability, utilization, innovation, effectiveness? Answers to these fundamental questions can help management focus the learning agenda on strategies that will maximize the development of business value for specific client segments.

The impact of information technology on learning will vary, depending upon the vision and the structure of individual organizations. From simple distributive technologies such as e-mail and presentation graphics to pervasive technologies and artificial intelligence, there appears to be little correlation between the sophistication of the technical infrastructure and an organization's ability to reach higher-level learning objectives. There is no 'one best way' of breeding corporate learning, but there is a need to ensure coherent choices between corporate vision, organizational structures and pertinent technical infrastructures.

The use of information technology to support learning will also depend upon how business value is being measured. As proposed in Chapter 3, 'Is What You Measure What You Get?', differing client metrics provide contrasting results. Profitability measures the added value of an organization in comparing the cost of its resources with that of the products and/or services. Quality can be defined variously as 'conformance to standards' as well as 'client satisfaction'. Innovation can be understood in the context of an organization's ability to react to real or perceived changes in the market or in the economy. Effectiveness can be viewed as an output–input ratio that addresses the question of 'doing the right things' to meet customer needs and objectives. Which use of information technology will best reflect the metrics your clients are using to judge your organization?

Finally, where in the organization can learning take place? The every-day routines and highly mechanical processes associated with the drive for efficiency leave little room for learning to innovate around new business challenges. Armed with the prescriptive remedies of working more quickly and cheaply, employees and partners alike will be challenged to make any sense of the often unstable and unstruc-tured environments of the joined-up economy. Beyond the light of the organizational structures and adapted best practices are organi-zational activities in which managers continue to explore new client demands and capitalize on past experience. In the shadows, informal networks are extremely helpful here in harnessing innovation and enthusiasm to help new solutions emerge and in minimizing the weight of existing norms and formal structures. Here the prescriptive nature of 'quicker, faster = better' gives way to vision, innovation and effectiveness. Information technology's impact on business value may also be greatest here in helping managers reconcile the organiza-tional demands for practical knowledge and acquired skills with the individual's needs for creativity and passion.

Notes

1. Chris Argyris makes a distinction between first-level and second-level learning. He argues that first-level learning consists of applying proven solutions to current challenges. In the event that these 'solutions' prove incapable of solving the problem, certain learners develop second-level learning in which they reframe the challenges to allow alternative solutions to emerge.
2. Synectics is an approach to creative thinking that depends on understanding together that which is apparently different. Its main tool is analogy or metaphor, using which, participants break existing mindsets and internalize abstract concepts. See Couch (1993).
3. A pilot project financed by the European Commission by means of an agreement with the Irish Productivity Centre (Ireland). Coordinated by the Tomillo Foundation's Centre for Economic Studies, the target population included SMEs in the United Kingdom, Italy, the Netherlands, Greece, Ireland, Germany, Finland, Portugal and Spain. See http://www.benchmarking-in-europe.com/.
4. Survey conducted by the present authors during the first Stresa Conference on Corporate Education, Stresa, Italy, 2001.
5. Once again, for the sake of simplicity, we have used the concept of 'actor' to refer both to individual actors and non-human 'actants' distinguished in 'actor network theory'. Both are potential sources of interaction costs. See Lin (2001).
6. The Doblin Group (www.doblin.com).

References

Couch, Richard (1993) Synectics and imagery: developing creative thinking through images. In *Art, Science and Visual Literacy*, Selected Readings from the 24th Annual Conference of the International Visual Literacy Association, Pittsburgh, PA, 30 September–4 October, 1992.

Drucker, F. P. (1998) Management's new paradigms, *Forbes*, 5 October, 152–177.

Hagel, John III, and Marc Singer (1999) Unbundling the corporation, *Harvard Business Review*, March–April.

Lewin, Kurt (1951) *Field Theory in Social Science*, New York: Harper & Row.

Lin, Nan (2001) *Social Capital: A Theory of Social Structure and Action*, Cambridge: Cambridge University Press.

Moe, Michael (2000) *The Knowledge Web: People Power – Fuel for the New Economy*, New York: Merrill-Lynch.

Stacy, Ralph (1995) *Strategic Management and Organizational Dynamics*, Hemel Hempstead: Prentice Hall.

The Effective
Organization

As a manager, your 'job' is adding value to your organization. Your contribution to your company, your profession and your career is based on client perceptions of the value of the products and services you have to offer. Perceptions of business value have changed significantly over the years in a joined-up economy where produced products, business processes and talent are no longer manufactured by any one firm but are co-designed, co-engineered and co-delivered by supply chains, networked firms and collaborative communities. In this light, we have tried to directly address the challenge of producing business value, and to outline practical strategies in building effective business organizations.

A number of conclusions can be drawn from our conversation. We suggest that improving business practice is not a 'packageable' solution but the core of corporate strategy. Business strategy should be based upon the company's convictions of the source of its value proposition, whether it is people, process or technology. When implementing corporate strategy you should pay close attention to where your stakeholders feel your efforts will be most effective: focusing on individual employees or managers, on teams, or on the market as a whole. The value of each proposal does not boil down to working more quickly and cheaply, but to a variety of value components ranging on a continuum from efficiency and utilization to quality, wisdom and effectiveness. These three axes form the basis of our Business Value Matrix™ which can help you understand how to develop value propositions consistent with the organization's culture and belief structure.

We suggest that there is no 'one best way' of using information technology to add value to business. Organizational investments in information technologies will impact, and be influenced by, investments in the key processes of the company. Technology and management are inherently intertwined: they cannot be analysed, implemented or optimized in isolation. Your current IT infrastructure provides a great deal of information about how work gets done (or fails to get done) inside your company and between your firm and its market. The gaps or inconsistencies in information, the bottlenecks in delivering information to your clients, indicate where and what employees, managers and business partners need to learn.

The overlap of information technology with management practice provides a mirror of company culture, vision and the prevailing principles of management theory. Similar to a house of mirrors, the introduction of PCs, relational databases, client/server systems and the Internet has offered contrasting definitions of where a business should focus its value propositions. Succeeding generations of information technology, based on concepts of personal productivity, the value chain, reengineering and the networked economy, have introduced different and sometimes contradictory demands on what individuals need to learn to survive, to compete and to prosper in a business environment. The potential tension between an individual's needs and beliefs and the organizational requirements reflected by each generation of information technology can help us understand why information technology has not led to greater increases in productivity.

We have argued that 'productivity' depends not only on how we measure performance but on the information technology we use to do so. We have suggested that the best intentions concerning information technology may lead to poor business practice. This tendency goes a long way to explaining why the introduction of information technology is often a source of intense anxiety for employees and managers alike. ICT can be seen as an acronym for how Individuals See Technology as management's attempt to enhance or minimize human resources; this view can contrast sharply with their individual passions, needs and objectives. Introducing new versions of technology, or enhancing product features, does not contribute to business value if it conflicts with the organization's values and beliefs, as well as with the individual's basic assumptions about the reality of work and the workplace.

The most significant contribution of information technology is in its capacity to push us to think differently about the relationship between what we measure and how we wish to improve our business practice. We have suggested three strategies for reconciling human endeavour, modern organizations and the market. One school of thought suggests strategies for influencing how we work by describing relevant 'skill sets' and relevant training strategies. A second school argues that managers must introduce new 'mindsets' concerning the workplace before employees will accept that they can change their skill sets. A third school argues that mindsets depend upon deeper-rooted collective beliefs about company culture, and that change management strategies need to begin by addressing the vision of what the company represents and how it wishes to develop.

The Business Value Matrix™ can help you identify factors that contribute to successful implementations of technology, as well as circumstances that tend to undermine these value propositions.

Individuals, teams and firms no longer work in isolation but within a 'joined-up economy' in which autonomous actors at all levels cooperate and compete for shared benefits. We have examined how the evolving relationship between strategy and customer needs has impacted learning communities within the company and between the firm and its external clients. We have analysed how the digitalization of key business processes has impacted the objectives and the structure of technology investments. We suggest that the characteristics of the joined-up economy impact the objectives, the form and the value of management in supporting innovation. These premises call out for a common understanding of business value, of how value is created in today's markets, and of how it can be enhanced in the future.

What do we need to learn to add value to our organizations? The everyday routines and/or highly mechanical processes inherent in our drive for corporate efficiency have added to our business challenges. Strengthening our formal structures of command and control have not provided adequate responses for dealing with either rapidly changing market conditions or rising levels of employee antipathy, anxiousness and stress. These formal structures of thought and organization must share the light with shadow, or informal, networks, which have proved to be better conduits of creativity, innovation and passion. In the shadows of our organization, the prescriptive nature of 'quicker, faster = better' gives way to vision, innovation and effectiveness. Information technology's impact on business value may also be greatest here, in illuminating the shadows of virtuous circles of talent, motivation and creativity in your organizations. In building a shared vision of business value for your organization, you can help to reconcile the organizational demands for practical knowledge and acquired skills with the individual's needs for creativity and passion.

In sum, we hope to have shed light on how you can breed business value into your projects, teams and organizations. The reality of the joined-up economy encourages us to focus on how we can work together with our clients and business partners to strengthen collaborative communities around a shared vision of the foundations of business value. A new generation of information technology, based on collaborative strategies, can be used to capture, store and communicate new metrics on the effectiveness of our relationships with internal and external clients. Built upon the foundations of 'efficiency', a new mindset around 'effectiveness' can help provide the nuts and bolts of business value for your professions, organizations and careers.

9 September, 2004

Lee Schlenker
Alan Matcham

Index